To Shirley Bain

TRUTH
IS NOT
PLURAL

Truth with a Capital
T

TRUTH
IS NOT
PLURAL

A RESPONSE TO THE "EXCLUSIVE"
PLURALISM OF JOHN HICK

ADDING AN "S" AFTER TRUTH
IS LIKE ADDING A "?" TO THE
ABSOLUTE LAWS OF PHYSICS

BY CONRAD L. NEUDORF

(B.R.E, M.T.S)

Xulon Press

Xulon Press
2301 Lucien Way #415
Maitland, FL 32751
407.339.4217
www.xulonpress.com

ISBN: 9781545604731

Dedicated To My Wife
Debbie

Without your love and partnership in marriage, I would not have been able to complete this daunting project. Your encouragement and self-sacrifice enabled me to have the courage to dream and imagine.

& To My Mother
Peggy (Margaret) 1932-2016

Her interest in writing and her constant belief in my abilities encouraged me to pursue this goal which, I did not consider possible.

Many Thanks To My Editors

Conrad Wiebe, Jean Neudorf, Stacey Rodway
and Rhona Neudorf

ENDORSEMENTS

This book is both a highly readable and creative discussion of a number of pressing questions in contemporary western culture. Readers will be given the opportunity to think again about such key concepts as the nature of truth, pluralism, revelation, and the true identity of Jesus of Nazareth. Neudorf combines an emphasis on the importance of truth with a helpful discussion of a number of the controversies it ignites in our culture. In the end, readers will be given new reasons to see Jesus as the very embodiment of truth and to have their own perspectives on truth clarified and broadened.

–Paul Chamberlain, Ph.D
Professor, Philosophy and Christian Apologetics,
Director, Institute of Christian Apologetics,
Trinity Western University (ACTS division)

Over 2000 years ago, a question was asked: "what is Truth?" Since then, a lot of answers have been given, and more than a few books have been written about it, including the one you are about to read.

I have known the author for over two years and believe me he can handle the Truth. "Truth Is Not Plural" will make you uncomfortable and it should. Do you think you can handle God as Truth?

–**Ben K. Cohen,**
Jewish Advisor.

"Every moral and ethical question boils down to one primary issue: "Is truth absolute or relative?" One option leads to clarity, hope and freedom while the other option leads to confusion, despair and bondage. The author boldly and passionately presents his compelling case that Jesus Christ is the embodiment of truth and that His existence as God incarnate establishes the reality of absolute truth. Truth is not nor ever can be plural. To embrace relativism is to deny the existence of God. The author surgically dissects the inner core of John Hicks arguments for relativism and exposes them as a theological cancer that can be halted with the radical therapy of God's self-revelation. In a time of significant moral confusion this book is a wake up call to church leaders. We must preach, teach and model an unapologetic confidence that Jesus Christ is TRUTH—full stop!"

–Rev. David Hearn,
President of the C&MA in Canada

TABLE OF CONTENTS

FOREWORD

onrad Neudorf is a close friend and confidant and I am very excited about his new book "Truth is Not Plural". It is a privilege and an honor to write this foreword for the book.

Throughout history humankind has been torn between two competing views of morality and truth, both of which exist at instinctive and almost primitive levels and which strain to mold our view of right versus wrong and true versus false. One of these views, posited by CS Lewis states, "conscience reveals to us a moral law whose source cannot be found in the natural world, thus pointing to the existence of a supernatural lawgiver" (God). The other of these views rejects this concept of a sovereign external standard of morality and truth, appealing instead to a perspective in which there are no moral or truth-based absolutes. Thus, morality and truth are relative to (or determined by) factors such as culture, societal influence, historical period, and even individual differences and preferences. Certain individuals hold exclusively to one or the other of these competing morality/truth perspectives, but in the name of those most human of traits – pragmatism and convenience, many apply whichever of these two models is best suited to the current situation at any given time. For example, when we encounter someone who intends to interfere with us or harm us, we naturally gravitate to the external moral perspective, asserting that their intension is morally wrong in an absolute and therefore irrefutable sense, and we hold to this position even when our assailant argues that their unique and relative moral perspective authorizes them to do as they wish. Conversely, when we wish to act in a manner which is for one reason or another questionable or controversial, we quickly appeal to the moral relativity model, boldly attesting that at this time and within the current context (relatively speaking), what we wish to do is in fact moral and just, at least for the time being. The tension between these two deep-seated and instinctive perspectives therefore persists, but Neudorf has recently waded into this debate, with this refreshing and highly relevant book.

Based upon his passion for God and comprehensive knowledge of scripture, Neudorf offers strong and compelling support for the concept of an external and absolute moral code and definition of truth, which as CS Lewis states "cannot be found in the natural world". However, Neudorf is at the same time respectful of the concept of personal freedom, which is a central tenant of the moral relativity perspective. More specifically, in reading this book, one has the sense that freedom is certainly a precious commodity, but in a system where truth is in fact absolute, the full experience of freedom can be achieved only by understanding and respecting those absolutes.

"Truth is Not Plural", is not only highly interesting, but is also a potentially very important read, dealing with a topic about which people have long searched and pondered, and offering advice and direction which could prove to be very helpful to those who have questions regarding this issue.

Dr. Myron G Schimpf Ph.D.
Psychology

PREFACE

CREED - BY STEVE TURNER

We believe in Marxfreudanddarwin.

We believe everything is OK

as long as you don't hurt anyone,

to the best of your definition of hurt,

and to the best of your knowledge.

We believe in sex before during

and after marriage.

We believe in the therapy of sin.

We believe that adultery is fun.

We believe that sodomy's OK.
We believe that taboos are taboo.

We believe that everything's getting better
despite evidence to the contrary.
The evidence must be investigated.
You can prove anything with evidence.

We believe there's something in horoscopes,
UFO's and bent spoons;
Jesus was a good man just like Buddha,
Mohammed and ourselves.
He was a good moral teacher although we think
his good morals were bad.

We believe that all religions are basically the same,
at least the one that we read was.
They all believe in love and goodness.
They only differ on matters of
creation sin heaven hell God and salvation.

We believe that after death comes The Nothing

because when you ask the dead what happens

they say Nothing.

If death is not the end, if the dead have lied,

then it's compulsory heaven for all

excepting perhaps Hitler, Stalin and Genghis Khan.

...We believe that man is essentially good.

It's only his behaviour that lets him down.

This is the fault of society.

Society is the fault of conditions.

Conditions are the fault of society...

We believe that each man must find the truth

that is right for him.

Reality will adapt accordingly.

The universe will readjust. History will alter.

We believe that there is no absolute truth

excepting the truth that there is no absolute truth...We believe in the rejection of creeds.[1]

WHAT IS TRUTH?

I believe that Truth always was, always is, and always will be. I believe that Truth was in the beginning with God, and that Truth is God. I believe that through Truth all things were made; without Truth nothing was made that has been made. I believe that in Truth was life, and that life was the light of humanity. Therefore, Jesus is Truth. I believe that "every worldview not based on Biblical Truth ends up with some form of reductionism. After all, if you do not begin with God, then you must begin with something less than God."[2] The quest for Truth is as ancient as the creation of humanity, and it resurfaces throughout history. No matter how many

1   Steve Turner, https://www.poemhunter.com/poem/creed/, Accessed March 7th, 2017, Copyright © 2003
2   Nancy Pearcey, *Total Truth: Liberating Christianity from Its Cultural Captivity,* 42.

philosophers, theologians, and modern thinkers grapple with its meaning, it is still a word that stirs emotion and controversy. Truth is powerful, because it is in essence more than just a word, an action, or merely a moral compass. I believe that the understanding of Truth has confused and alluded *eluded* so many thinkers in our society, because its meaning can be found only as the embodiment of a Person - The Creator of all - not merely as a moral guide relative to one's culture.

Therefore I would propose that if in fact "Truth" is God, then this word must be singular, because if Truth has an "s" at the end, its meaning is altered and becomes a contradiction. The One who is the Alpha and Omega, the Beginning and the End, the One who was and is and is yet to come, is the very embodiment of "Truth." Truth is therefore not plural; it is singular. *In fact, to add an "s" at the end of Truth would be like adding a "?" at the end of the absolute laws of physics.*

One of my favourite modern philosophers, Francis Schaeffer, was known for holding to account the godless culture of his age and for confronting the hypocrisy within the church community. He was bold for Christ and made clear the false ideologies and philosophies permeating his culture. In that vein, he gave an address to the young minds at the University of Notre Dame and noted, "Christianity is not a series of truths in the plural, but rather truth spelled with a capital "T". Truth about total reality, not just about religious things. Christianity, Biblical Christianity, is Truth concerning total reality and the intellectual holding of that total Truth and then living in the light of that truth."[3]

Absolute Truth provides humanity with purpose and meaning for our lives. It exists as a foundation upon which we choose right from wrong, upon which laws will govern our society, and which answers the most fundamental questions we face regarding life and death. Without Truth the world becomes confused and disunified, ultimately producing anarchism. Linda Keffer from Focus on the Family says that without absolute Truth

---

[3] Francis Schaeffer, Address at the University of Notre Dame, April 1981.

"we are alone and it is every man for himself. And we're without a purpose; if there's no true story of where we came from and why we're here, then there's nothing that really gives our lives meaning."[4]

Our society has become so confused about the definition of Truth that the meaning has in many ways become irrelevant. In fact, our culture has invented a new word to describe how the postmodern, millennial views "Truth." Recently CNN announced that "The Oxford Dictionary's Word of the Year 2016 is *post-truth* – an adjective defined as 'relating to or denoting circumstances in which objective facts are less influential in shaping public opinion than appeals to emotion and personal belief'."[5]

I believe that when Truth can no longer be distinguished from a lie or when one cannot trust what is said

[4] Lindy Keffer, http://www.focusonthefamily.com/parenting/teens/absolute-truth, Internet; Accessed November 18, 2016.Copyright © 2000 Focus on the Family, Originally titled "Ultimate Truth: Discovering Absolutes in a 'Whatever' World."
[5] CNN News, https://en.oxforddictionaries.com/word-of-the-year-2016, Internet; Accessed November 18, 2016.

to be the absolute Truth, society will eventually break-down. Ravi Zacharias shared a story which reveals what happens when the foundations of absolute Truth disintegrate.

> *"A few weeks ago, I did a lectureship at Ohio State University. As I was being driven to the lecture, we passed the new Wexner Art Center. The driver said, "This is a new art building for the university. It is a fascinating building designed in the post-modernist view of reality." The building has no pattern. Staircases go nowhere. Pillars support nothing. The architect designed the building to reflect life. It went nowhere and was mindless and senseless. I turned to the man describing it and asked, "Did they do the same thing with the foundation?" He laughed. You can't do that with a foundation. You can get away with the infrastructure.*

You can get away with random thoughts
that sound good in defense of a worldview
that ultimately doesn't make sense. Once
you start tampering with the foundations,
you begin to see the serious effects. Yet the
foundations are in jeopardy; the founda-
tions of our culture do not provide coherent
sets of answers any more.[6]

One of the earliest Christian apologists, St. Augustine described what happens when absolute Truth is compromised. He states, "When regard for truth has broken down or even slightly weakened, all things will remain doubtful."[7] Everything remains doubtful because Truth demands to be absolute or it becomes a lie. Stretch it even a micro millimeter and everything crumbles because the very foundation has been compromised

---

[6]   Ravi Zacharias [What About the Foundation?, *"If the Foundations Be Destroyed,"* Preaching Today, Tape No. 142
[7]   Augustine: *Treatises on Various Subjects*, Edited by Roy J. Deferrari, (Catholic University of America Press, INC., Washington, D.C. 1952), 78.

and thus disintegrates. Ralph Keyes points out what todays understanding of truth looks like in his book *The Post-Truth Era*, "In the post-truth era we don't just have truth and lies, but a third category of ambiguous statements that are not exactly the truth but fall short of a lie. Enhanced truth it might be called. Neo-truth. Soft-truth. Faux-truth. Truth-lite."[8] How can something be "not exactly the truth"? We shall discover that if the Truth is not absolute, if the Truth cannot stand on its own, it is simply a lie. Now lies may vary in severity; however, the outcome remains the same: it is still a lie. Yet, for the Truth to be 100%, it must come from a source that is also 100% pure, or holy. Therefore, I propose that 100% Truth must be God, and since Jesus Christ claimed to be the embodiment of the Truth, then we must assume He is God. "Jesus said to the people who believed in him, "You are truly my disciples if you remain faithful to my

---

[8] Ralph Keyes, The Post-Truth Era: *Dishonesty and Deception in Contemporary Life,* (St. Martin's Press, New York, 2004), 15.

teachings. And you will know the truth, and the truth will set you free." (John 8:31-32) NLT

If Jesus Himself said that He is the embodiment of the Truth/God, then everything that flows from Him is the Truth in action. This logically would mean that if the Bible is God's Word and if Jesus is God incarnate, then everything in the Holy Scriptures is the Truth, because it not only comes from God but is the Living Word/Truth. Yet, there are many in our postmodern society that would argue that Truth cannot be absolute, especially in one person and even more unlikely if this person is Jesus Christ. They would argue that Jesus never claimed to be God incarnate and that there is no evidence that He is Truth. This book will present solid evidence that if Jesus Christ is God, He is therefore the only One who embodies Truth. If this is reality, the concept of pluralism must be seen as a contradiction, which cannot be lived out and must be seen as a lie.

In this book I have chosen to respond to one particular philosopher by the name of John Hick who has written many books arguing against the divinity of Jesus Christ and who presents a pluralistic supposition that truth is relative to one's culture. He argues that "god" is not a knowable person but an unknowable reality - an "it." I will attempt to show the logic of traditional Christianity's continued belief in Jesus as the only personification of the Truth, the whole Truth and nothing but the Truth. It is my belief that John Hick's pluralistic definition of the word "Truth" is a philosophical contradiction, not only because it erodes the very meaning of the word, But that it also denies the very existence of God/Truth. We will discover that Truth must be absolute in all things including our religious worldview. The only time John Hick and other pluralistic debaters believe in exclusivity is when they claim that the pluralistic belief must be, in itself, exclusive. They believe exclusively that the word truth must have an "s" on the end.

Questions generated by the dissonance between traditional Christian beliefs in the exclusivity of Christ and contemporary Western society's acceptance of pluralism have created some of the most important challenges facing the church doctrinally, theologically and philosophically within the twenty-first century. Thus, the contemporary but still traditional Christian community must become more vigilant in providing answers for those who would challenge the centrality of Jesus, which is the cornerstone of Christianity. C. S. Lewis warned,

> *To be ignorant and simple now - not to be able to meet the enemies on their own ground - would be to throw down our weapons, and to betray our uneducated brethren who have under God, no defense but us against the intellectual attacks of the heathen. Good philosophy must exist, if for no other reason, because bad philosophy needs to be answered.* [9]

[9] C. S. Lewis, *The Weight of Glory and Other Addresses* (New York: Macmillian, 1980), 28.

My primary focus will be theological; however I will also incorporate a philosophical and apologetic approach. I am assuming that a religious study of any kind must not be based solely on one discipline, but must combine various fields of study. Author Donald G. Bloesch asserts, "The task of theology is to articulate the message of faith in the conceptuality of the age while at the same time bringing this conceptuality under the searing critique of divine revelation."[10] Furthermore he states, "Theology is free to use philosophical terminology in order to elucidate biblical meanings, but it must not become bound to this terminology."[11] These disciplines view God from different perspectives and thus need to be addressed in the study of religion.

It is important to note that the God of the First and Second Covenant (Old Testament & New Testament) makes Himself known through Jesus Christ who embodies the Word (Holy Scriptures) and by the Holy

---

[10] Donald G. Bloesch, *God The Almighty: Power, Wisdom, Holiness, Love* (Downers Grove: Inter-Varsity Press, 1995), 29.
[11] Ibid., 32.

Spirit who embodies the regenerated believer. Bloesch would agree and states, "The God of philosophy is capable of being thought and thereby mastered. The God of theology remains hidden and inscrutable until he makes Himself known."[12] Yet, there are those that continue to add, twist, tangle, redact, distort, and confuse the Word of Truth. Enemies of the Truth/God will continue to call Truth a lie and a lie the Truth until the return of Jesus Christ; but then they, like everyone else, will bow before Him. "Therefore, God elevated him to the place of highest honour and gave him the name above all other names, that at the name of Jesus every knee should bow, in heaven and on earth and under the earth, and every tongue confess that Jesus Christ is Lord, to the glory of God the Father." (Philippians 2:9-11)

This book will respond to a few primary objections that philosopher John Hick levels against Christianity's traditional doctrine of Jesus as the embodiment of the absolute Truth. My intent agrees with a statement

---

[12] Ibid.

made by Gregory Cruthers where he says, "…given Christianity's contemporary interaction with world faiths," is to more deeply "understand from within the standpoint of Christian faith some aspects of the mystery of who Jesus is."[13] Therefore, my goal for those who are wrestling with the age old question "What is Truth?" is that in time they will discover that this word is singular, and that Jesus is the *only one* who can forgive sins and offer a relationship with the Father. It is my prayer that the reader will come to know Jesus as Truth and the only one capable of bringing them joy, peace, hope, and eternal life.

My primary objective will be to provide the reader with evidence that Jesus is the embodiment of the Way, the Truth, and the Life and to provide a response to a number of counter claims that John Hick has made. Hick believes that Jesus was only one of many truth's,' and that

---

[13] Gregory H. Carruthers, *The Uniqueness of Jesus Christ in the Theocentric Model of the Christian Theology of World Religions: An Elaboration and Evaluation of the Position of John Hick* (Lanham: University Press of America, Inc. 1990), 3.

He was a good man who was able to draw people to the "Ultimate Real." Through his writings we can determine that he believes that Jesus is merely one of many metaphorical incarnations rather than the literal and unique incarnation of God the Father. It is my prayer that you will recognize the urgent need to justify this historic Christian doctrine of absolute Truth and to reject the false and powerless doctrine of pluralism.

It is very important for today's Christian Church to affirm this essential historic Christian doctrine. Without it, the world will be lost and without hope. If Jesus is brought down to being only one of many ways to salvation, the Christian Church, as the mystical body of Christ, will bear no fruit, provide no hope, and sustain no spiritual life. It will essentially die a slow death. This book is a warning to the evangelical church which is in danger of becoming powerless in this age of relativism and unbelief if it does not become more emboldened to speak about the Truth of the gospel in absolute terms.

Schaeffer already saw this coming many years ago when he stated,

> *"Here is the great evangelical disaster – the failure of the evangelical world to stand for truth as truth. There is only one word for this – accommodation: the evangelical church has accommodated to the world spirit of the age.... Truth carries with it confrontation. Truth demands confrontation: loving confrontation, but confrontation nevertheless. If our reflex action is always accommodation regardless of the centrality of the truth involved, there is something wrong."[14]*

I assume that those holding to a postmodern pluralistic worldview may label me as an "intolerant right–wing Christian" attempting to justify my evangelical,

---

[14] Francis Schaeffer, *The Evangelical Disaster*, (Crossway Books, 1300 Crescent Street, Wheaton Illinois, 1984), 37.

fundamentalist dogma of Truth, and they would be absolutely correct. Yet, my motives are based on a love for humanity and a desire for them to follow the Truth/ Jesus to find relationship and peace with the Father. Geivett suggests for today's postmodern mind, "The mere suggestion that Jesus might be the *only* way to achieve authentic religious fulfillment smacks of bigoted narrowness and rigid exclusiveness."[15] Today's western society must bring back to its universities and colleges the love of reason, logic and debate without having to resort to name calling and to allowing a voice only to those with whom they agree. I understand that the message of Jesus has never been the most popular and politically correct throughout history. Jesus was often accused of going against the mainstream and being rather intolerant.

I believe that it is precisely because of this reverse intolerance and lack of understanding in our society that

---

[15] Douglas R.Geivett, "Is Jesus the Only Way?" in Michael J. Wilkins and J. P. Moreland (eds.) *Jesus Under Fire* (Grand Rapids: Zondervan Publishing House, 1995), 178.

the question regarding whether or not Truth is singular must be asked. Addressing this issue is also essential for the local church community because pluralism and universalism have influenced so many pastors, priests, church leaders, and traditional Christians to doubt and, in some cases, abandon the true historical position of exclusivity in Jesus. Hick believes that many leaders within the World Council have already made a theological paradigm shift, contending that "The Christian mind has now for the most part made the move from an intolerant exclusivism to a benevolent inclusivism."[16]

Hick has led the way towards the growing belief that "There is not merely one way but a plurality of ways of salvation or liberation . . . taking place in different ways within the contexts of all the great religious traditions."[17] Undoubtedly, his statement that the church needs to focus more on learning about the relationship

---

[16] John Hick, "The Non-Absolutism of Christianity." in John Hick and, Paul F. Knitter (eds.), *The Myth of Christian Uniqueness* (New York: Orbis Books, 1987), 22.
[17] Ibid.

between Christianity and world religions is correct, since non-Christian faiths are no longer only in distant lands but are now within Western society. Yet in doing so, we must stand firm on the teaching of Jesus, who has revealed to us that He is the only Truth that can save humanity from their innate desire towards self-worship. He is the only one that can fix this broken world and bring restoration and peace that will pass all understanding. Carruthers agrees that, "If the church is to advance in learning as it explores this new field [world religions], it will not be able to do so by abandoning the truth that it has already learned correctly."[18]

As we closely examine Hick's inclusive worldview which gives birth to pluralism, I want to challenge you to observe what he is really saying. I want you to notice that his view is not quite as "tolerant" as he would like you to believe. Hick professes that every religion must

---

[18] Gregory H. Carruthers, S. J., The Uniqueness of Jesus Christ in the Theocentric Model of the Christian Theology of World Religions: An Elaboration and Evaluation of the Position of John Hick (Lanham: University Press of America, Inc. 1990), 2.

eventually come into his pluralistic camp. Yet, I know from personal experience that if a person of one faith chooses to opt out of the pluralist band-wagon, he or she will be quickly labeled an intolerant bigot who has chosen the lower moral road. According to Hick, all faiths *must* begin to move away from being self-centered (i.e., focused on a particular religious theology such as Jesus Himself as the personification of the Truth) to being centered on the "Ultimate Real." Yet this begs the question, who is being exclusive now? I even question the logic of being an exclusive pluralist? Is it even possible for someone to actually say that they believe that pluralism is the "ONLY WAY" or that eventually we must ALL evolve or shift towards that direction? Is it not obvious that we live in a world of absolutes and that we all rely on natural and moral laws to be true everyday? If we rely on absolute truths in every other discipline involving our life, why would we not assume that this must also be the case with the discipline of religion? My point is, that if the laws of nature are absolute, logic would assume that the One who created these laws would also be Truth personified. I will try to persuade you, or at least provide you with evidence that Truth exists as the personification of a great being, namely Jesus Christ, who claimed to BE THAT TRUTH. I propose that if there is more than one Truth, there must be more than one being that embodies Truth. Yet, this type of flawed logic leads down the crooked road of contradiction, which transforms into a lie.

If all the ideologies, religions, and philosophies which contradict each other claim to be the Truth, then it would be logical to say that all but one are actually liars. If Jesus is the personification of the Truth, then all other truth claims come from the father of lies (the devil). In John 8:44 Jesus says, "For you are the children of your father the devil, and you love to do the evil things that He does. He was a murderer from the beginning. He has always hated "THE TRUTH" because there is NO TRUTH in him. When he lies, it is consistent with his character; for he is a liar and the father of lies." (NLT)

This passage clearly states that the devil is not only the personification of the word "lie," but that all his actions are lies. The Truth or God is not in him. Therefore, we can say that at its genesis, Truth exists as a Higher Being where every action and reaction gives birth to Truth. This Being/God must then exist as the absolute foundation upon which all the actions of humanity are procured. This Being must also be the foundation for humanity's behavior towards the One who is Truth, towards each other, and towards all creatures He has made (The Law). In other words, for absolute Truth to be found we must begin at the beginning and look at the One in whose image humanity has been created - Imago Dei.

It is Hick's conviction that any faith holding to an exclusivity doctrine is false. Yet if that is correct, even his claim would be unwarranted and inappropriate in this modern era. He says, "In light of our accumulated knowledge of the other great world faiths, [Christian exclusivism] has become unacceptable to all except a minority of dogmatic diehards."[19] Yet, this "accumulated knowledge" from his worldview also sounds rather exclusive, does it not? It is common knowledge that if one is to maintain a belief system, it must be also affirmed. However, in affirming one's own belief, a rejection of an opposing belief system has already occurred, thus making the one belief rejected a lie, and the one accepted as the absolute truth. This would mean that any belief system would be particular or exclusive in nature. In fact, every human being has a particular worldview and a faith in something and is therefore exclusive.

You will notice that Hick's hypothesis is no exception to this logic. His new definition of God dictates everything within his worldview, and totally contradicts traditional Christianity's doctrine of the source of Truth coming from Jesus Christ. Logic and mere reason tells us that only one Being can exist as the personification and source of Truth. This Being must then be **all**

---

[19] John Hick, *God Has Many Names* (Philadelphia: Westminster, 1982), 27.

powerful, **all** knowing, **all** present, **all** holy and pure. There cannot be more than one Being that is the Great "I AM", and who exists as the All in All. Jesus knew who He was when he so clearly stated that He is the "Way, the Truth, and the Life," and then in words absolute said, "... no one comes to the Father except by Me." (John 3:16) Therefore, without Jesus, every worldview, philosophy, religion, and ideology must be false. Truth is not tolerant. That is why it is True.

Ravi Zacharias believes that in today's society it is difficult to communicate the concept that anything can be exclusive. He states that, "Philosophically, you can believe anything, as long as you do not claim it to be true. Morally, you can believe anything, so long as you do not claim that it is a better way. Religiously, you can hold to anything, so long as you don't bring Jesus into it."[20]

While Hick's so-called solution to the issue of the uniqueness of Jesus Christ appeals to some, his

---

[20] Ravi Zacharias, *Jesus Among Other Gods: The Absolute Claims of the Christian Message* (Nashville: W. Publishing Group, 2000), vii.

hypothesis fails to be convincing enough to abandon Jesus as Truth. Carruthers asserts that Hick's solution "neither represents a faithful explanation of the origins of how the church came to learn of the uniqueness of Jesus, nor does it offer a faithful advance in the reinterpretation of that Christian affirmation."[21] On the other hand, if it can be conclusively demonstrated that Jesus did not claim His own deity, it would be highly plausible that He was not God incarnate (the embodiment of Truth) and that the church is continuing to believe what is historically inaccurate. So, if Truth is not found in the embodiment of a Greater Personal Being, then I am afraid that life contradicts itself simply because humanity's built-in desire and pursuit of absolute "Truth" would not exist, and yet it does. The question is, why?

---

[21] Gregory H. Carruthers, S. J., *The Uniqueness of Jesus Christ in the Theocentric Model of the Christian Theology of World Religions, An Elaboration and Evaluation of the Position of John Hick* (Lanham: University Press of America, Inc. 1990).

I believe the answer is right in front of us, and this is why a discussion regarding absolute Truth is so very important in the midst of today's relativistic worldview. Sadly, our Western society has become so intolerant of any view which differs from its own that many institutions of higher education won't allow one to express one's view without ridicule. In fact, if you hold to a view which differs from the mainstream liberal agenda of radical inclusivism, your voice will be drowned out—not with counter arguments of reason, but with mocking and condescending words of self-righteousness. Thus, I believe it is imperative that we provide convincing evidence and reason for those who still hold to a belief in the deity of Jesus as the absolute Truth.

To accomplish these goals I have laid out a concise summary and strategy which will be your guide to how I will attempt to arrive at my conclusion that Jesus is Truth without an "s."

SUMMARY AND STRATEGY

1. Radical Understanding of Truth

Chapter one will set the stage for the next eight chapters. I will show that the representation of Truth must always be undergirded by love and be delivered with an attitude of respect, for all are made in the image of God. We will look at the radical understanding that Truth is the personification of Jesus Christ who exists as God incarnate and that everything emanating from Him such as His words, His actions, and His judgments - will be Truth. We will see that the law demands this Truth and that without a law there is no dispensing of the Truth in a sinful world. If the law does not have as its foundation God/Truth, there will be nothing left to judge. We will also define some phrases and words such as warranted belief, traditional Christian, absolutism, exclusivity and particularism.

2. Why John Hick

I believe that it is important to begin chapter two describing who John Hick is and why I chose this particular pluralist to rebut in this study on Truth. In order to know the process by which he began his pluralistic hypothesis we must have some knowledge regarding his family life and influences including his places education. We must also know which various philosophers and theologians influenced his worldview. We will learn what led to his decision to move from a Christocentric exclusive worldview to a pluralistic understanding of world religions. I will reveal in his own words why he felt he could no longer believe that Jesus is the personification of Truth (God incarnate).

3. John Hick's Truth's' Hypothesis

In chapter three I will provide a short version of John Hick's pluralistic hypothesis, which gradually developed into two primary stages. The first stage is Hick's Copernican revolution, wherein he moves from a Christocentric to a Theocentric theology; in the second stage he moves from a Theocentric theology to a more encompassing salvation/liberation centered theology of world religions. The influence of Immanuel Kant and his epistemological model on Hick's development of the concept of the unknowable "Real" will also be traced. Finally, I will close the chapter with an explanation of the grading system that Hick applies in order to decide which world religions can be categorized as being based on the "Ultimate Real."

4. John Hick's Objections

In chapter four I will examine two of Hick's primary objections to the deity of Jesus/Truth as asserted by traditional Christianity. Hick is well aware that if he demonstrates that the theology of the literal incarnation was developed, all the Christocentric doctrines of traditional Christianity will totally collapse. If the incarnation did not occur, then Jesus is not God and the self-claim passages of Jesus referring to His deity are not authentic. Thus, Hick's first objection is to assert that Jesus never claimed His own Deity (incarnation), but that His followers conferred it upon Him. His second objection ascertains that the deity doctrine (incarnation) of Jesus gradually developed within the church, moving from deification of Jesus to the final Trinitarian belief of Father, Son, and Holy Spirit.

5. Historical Affirmations of Jesus As Truth

Chapter five begins with vital background evidence that will enable my response to Hick's arguments in this chapter. Hick's assertion that the self-claim passages of Jesus were the result of writers adding theological words to deify Jesus sixty to seventy years after his death must be immediately challenged. First, we will take a closer look at the passages that Hick believes were added by later writers. He asserts that these insertions contributed to the development of a theology that resulted in the deification of Jesus at the Council of Nicaea. In addition, we will study the central self-claim passages of Jesus, including verses from the gospels that reveal His pre-existence, exclusivity, deity, incarnation, as well as passages referring to the worship of Jesus as God. Once the primary Scriptures have been observed, testimonial evidence will be examined. Testimony will be presented from early believers, including the martyrs, the early church fathers, and early creed confessions revealing the worship of Jesus as God.

I will show that the church did not deify Jesus over time by placing words into His mouth, because the testimony of the early believers in the oral tradition, their actions and written documents counter that claim. This disapproval, or at least, weakening, of Hick's foundational reasons for rejecting certain doctrines, words, passages, and scriptural books will strengthen chapter six's response to Hick's two objections against the exclusive incarnation of Jesus.

6. Contemporary Response to Hick's Objections

The intent of chapter six will be to show that Hick does not have sufficient evidence to warrant his removal of Christocentric doctrines from the Christian faith. This chapter will affirm and defend the exclusive doctrine of the incarnation of Jesus Christ as literal and thus historical. Evidence will be provided showing that Jesus shouted out His own deity in Scripture, as He revealed His authority over creation, performing supernatural events, culminating in His resurrection. I will show that the teaching of the incarnation and subsequent doctrines were not products of overly zealous followers, but a result of the historical reality that changed their lives. The followers of Jesus were transformed, both inside and out, by the presence of Jesus, both before and after His resurrection. This change led to their mission to go into all the world and preach the gospel of the Jesus of history and faith. Their belief that Jesus was Truth is what led to their martyrdom and to subsequent doctrinal definitions within the church.

7. Additional Evidence that Jesus is Truth

In chapter seven we will discover additional evidence that Jesus is the personification of the Truth with a capital T. The early church members followed theological doctrines already believed by the disciples through oral tradition and the written word. In this chapter we are going to discover some primary evidence that reveals Jesus as the Truth including examples of eyewitness testimonies, and even an argument of credulity represented by the apostles own conversion experience. We will look at some of the flaws of John Hick's attempts at form, source and redaction criticism. We conclude chapter seven by revealing major flaws within the various Jesus seminars by comparing their findings with the sound discipline of the oral tradition.

8. Conclusion and Summary

I will conclude with a summary in chapter eight and assess the objections and arguments of Hick's hypothesis, comparing them with the arguments of this book. I will reveal that the Jesus presented in the New Testament is the same Jesus the early church loved and worshiped as God/Truth. I will conclude that, based on the evidence, Jesus is the personification of the Truth and that Truth is not a valid word if it has an "s" at the end.

CHAPTER ONE

A RADICAL UNDERSTANDING OF TRUTH

"Yes, if truth is not undergirded by love, it makes the possessor of that truth obnoxious and the truth repulsive."

– Ravi Zacharias

A RADICAL
UNDERSTANDING
OF TRUTH

WHAT TRUTH IS

Sir Arthur Conan Doyle's fictitious character, Sherlock Holmes, made a profound statement on how one can discover Truth. He was discussing the latest case with his assistant, Dr. Watson, when Sherlock chastises him, "How often have I said to you when you have eliminated the impossible, whatever remains, *however improbable*, must be the truth? We know that he did not come through the door, the window, or the chimney. We also know that he could not have been concealed in the room, as there is no concealment possible. When, then, did he come?"[22]

Sherlock's goal was to look for absolute Truth wherever it took him because the dispensing of justice depended on it. In the same way that God is always there, Truth is ever present, but in a world corrupted by evil and lies Truth must be sought out from within the eyes of God. Jesus Himself claimed to be not only the absolute Truth but its very essence - its very embodiment. He claimed that the definition of that word is not only in Him, but that it is Him, and that without Him there can be no Truth in action. Jesus consistently claimed to be the flesh of God. In fact He said, "I and the Father are one" (John 10:30, NASB) Jesus also claimed, "He who has seen Me has seen the Father..." (John 14:9b, NASB), Jesus did not give Christians (followers of Jesus) any other option but to preach that it is only through faith in His sacrificial death on Calvary that the world can

---

[22] Sir Arthur Conan Doyle, *Sherlock Holmes in: The Sign of the Four*, (Doubleday 1890) p.111.

receive forgiveness from its sins. Absolute Truth! Jesus told us, "I am the Way, the Truth, and the Life. No one can come to the Father except through me," (John 14: 6, NLT). Absolute Truth! Jesus claimed to be God, and since God is Truth, love in action becomes proof that He is Truth. Ravi Zacharias reveals that Truth delivered without love will produce dead fruit. "Yes, if truth is not undergirded by love, it makes the possessor of that truth obnoxious and the truth repulsive."[23] This quote supports the apostle John's words when he explains, "God showed how much He loved us by sending His only Son into the world so that we might have eternal life through Him. This is real love (which proves He is the Truth). It is not that we loved Him, but that He loved us and sent His Son as a sacrifice to take away our sins." (1 John 4:9-10).

---

[23] Lee Strobel, *A Case For Faith: A Journalist Investigates the Toughest Questions of the Christian Faith*, (Zondervan, Grand Rapids, Michigan, 2000), p150. Quoting Ravi Zacharias, Jesus Among Other gods: The Absolute Claims of the Christian Message.

This absolute love is given as a gift to all humanity. A pure act of grace dependent on nothing we can do other than to believe, receive, and follow the Saviour. This is not a fickle love that is relatively dependent on a situation, attitude, or on the cultural or religious environment in which one has been raised up. Anyone claiming to be the Truth or to have the Truth, but is not the One True God of the Bible, is a liar and the "Truth" is not in him/her. The proof that God is the "Truth" is in the fact that He also exists as "Love" and personally sacrificed Himself (Jesus Christ) to free humanity from the slavery of sin and rose from the dead to reveal His superiority over death and give us life. Any other belief, ideology, or religion is thereby an absolute lie because the "Truth" is not plural. Every human being must eventually make a decision whether or not the statements Jesus made about Himself are the Truth or a lie. There is no middle ground or relativity in His statements. Truth is not Truth if it has an "s" added at the end.

Still, there are those in our culture who preach that Truth is relative to the Environment in which they live or the situation in which they find themselves. Some have even suggested that Truth is relative to one's own interpretation of that so called Truth. It is almost as if the world has become schizophrenic, believing in one thing and yet daily living out the opposite. On the one hand, the world is searching for Truth and wants it to be singular when involving justice, love, and the natural laws of science. On the other hand, they can not accept the possibility that the God of the Bible and His laws of metaphysics are Truth in the singular.

Many in today's society are asking the question that if God exists as the Truth, then why does He not do something about "evil" to prove His existence. C.S. Lewis describes his struggle with this question in *Mere Christianity*, "My argument against God was that the universe seemed so cruel and unjust. But how had I got this idea of just and unjust? A man does not call a line crooked unless he has some idea of a straight line.

What was I comparing this universe with when I called it unjust."[24]

Another important question must be asked in order to find the answer. Why does evil exist at all? And if there is no God, then who will judge the evil that does exist? Interestingly, our society does not want Christianity's understanding of God (Truth) to be the final judge as to what the definition of evil should look like. Surprisingly, the answer to the problem of evil resides in the fact that God is the personification of Truth. In order for God to perfectly judge evil, He must be the very definition of Truth, which is the source of all that is good. Absolute evil can be judged only by absolute Truth. So how does a world without God respond to this dilemma? They deny His existence because He allows evil to exist, and at the same time they do not want to believe in a God who would decide for them what defines what is good, evil, truth, or lies. What the world really wants is to be

---

[24] Lewis, C.S. *Mere Christianity*, (HarperSanFrancisco, Zondervan Publishing House, 1952), 38.

the primary judge and creator so that it can decide who or what God/Truth is. They are then saying that they are god, they are the truth, and that they are the absolute judge. This is the same attitude which caused the fall of humanity in Genesis.

Humanity still wants to do what is right in its own eyes. Thus they want to be free from God/Truth. When we decide to choose our own way, our fate is sealed and sin enters our world. Proverbs 14:12 reminds us all that, "There is a way that seems right to a man, but its end is the way to death." Therefore the world's indecision becomes its ultimate decision that God and absolute Truth do not exist. They will propagate and guard this demonic belief by any means. This reminds me of something Michael Rivero said: "The truth is 'hate speech' only to those who have something to hide."[25]

---

[25] Rivero, Michael, "Hate Speech' And The massive Israeli US Spying Operation." Available from http://rense.com/general24/spy.htm, Internet; accessed, January 6th 2016.

WHAT TRUTH IS NOT

Many times a word becomes easier to understand when you look at the negative of that word. There is no Truth apart from Jesus Christ. If God is the personification of the Truth, then Truth can exist only if God exists. The Truth is not in the devil. There is no truth in any of his actions or in anything that comes out of his mouth because he is the personification of lies. I quoted earlier from the Scriptures that the devil is the father of lies and therefore is the opposite of the Truth (God). I want to share with you the lyrics of a great song written in the 70's by one of my favorite Christian musicians and authors, the late Keith Green. In this example Keith describes perfectly the character and actions of the one who embodies the word "lie."

No One Believes in Me Anymore or "The Devil's Boast."

Well, my job keeps getting easier as time keeps slipping away. I can imitate the brightest light, and make your night look just like day. I put some truth in every lie to tickle itching ears. I'm drawing people just like flies, 'cause they like what they hear. I'm gaining power by the hour; they're falling by the score. It's getting very simple now, since no one believes in me anymore.

Heaven's just a state of mind," my books read on your shelf. Have you heard that God is dead? I made that one up myself! They're dabbling in magic spells; they get their fortunes read. They heard the truth, but turned away and followed me instead. I used to have to sneak around, but now they just open their doors. No one's watching for my tricks, since no one believes in me anymore.

Everyone likes a winner - with my help, you're guaranteed to win. Hey, man, you're not a sinner - no, you've got the truth within. And as your life slips by, you'll believe the lie that you did it on your own. But I'll be there to help you share a dark eternal home.

My job keeps getting easier as day slips into day. The magazines, the newspapers print every word I say. This world is just my spinning top; it's all like child's play. I dream that it will never stop, but I know it's not that way. Still my work goes on and on, always stronger than before. I'm going to make it dark before the dawn, since no one believes in me anymore.[26]

---

[26] Keith Gordon Green/ Melody Green, No One Believes In Me Anymore. Lyrics © 1977, Sony/ATV Music Publishing, LLC.

Having the origin of the word "lie" in mind, let's take a look at six points from Norman Geisler as to what the word "truth" is not.

1. *Truth is not what works. This is pragmatism – an ends vs. means type approach. The reality is, lies can appear to "work", but they are still lies.*

2. *Truth is not what is coherent or understandable. A group of people can get together and form a conspiracy based on a set of falsehoods where they all agree to tell the same false story, but it does not make their presentation true.*

3. *Truth is not what makes people feel good. Unfortunately, bad news can be true.*

4. *Truth is not what the majority says is true. The fact is 51% of a group can reach a wrong or false conclusion.*

5. *Truth is not what is comprehensive. A very detailed and long presentation can still reach a false end result.*

6. *Truth is not what is intended. A good intention can still be wrong.*[27]

---

[27] Norman Geisler, "Truth, Nature of" in Baker Encyclopedia of Christian Apologetics (Grand Rapids, MI: 1999), 741-2.

THE LAW AND ABSOLUTE TRUTH

I had a discussion with a young man a number of years ago at a Wellness Fair. Our church had been invited to have a booth at this annual event. The "religious event" in the guise of a Wellness Fair had a plethora of so called "scientific" booths including a few representing New Age pluralism, tarot card readers, and astrologists. A young man from the New Age table came to our booth and we entered into a discussion about Truth. I asked Him if he believed in the existence of One supreme God who is the Personification of Truth. This young millenial responded with an answer that is quite common in today's spiritually interested and yet confused culture. He said, "Absolute Truth may be fine for you, and I am so glad that your truth works for you, but I hold to a different kind of truth." I responded by asking him if he believed in pluralism absolutely. He seemed in a hurry to leave, but our discussion ended as most conversations do in today's non-reasoning society. He said,

"Truth is different for everyone. I have my own belief and I don't appreciate you challenging it or suggesting that I am wrong." He did not want to discuss, debate, or even reason with me. Author Art Lindsley says, "Some cultural forms of tolerance minimize the differences among views. If your religion is merely true for you and my religion true for me, then what we believe is a matter of arbitrary personal preference. Truth is not at issue here."[28] It would be interesting to know if this young man really believed what he said with all his heart? Would he be willing to die for truth with an "s" which is a contradiction in and of itself? Would he want a court of law to use that same definition of Truth when he was looking for absolute justice?

The world continues to define and in some cases deny sin, evil, truth, and lies in its own relative terms rather than God's absolute terms, because it is human nature not ever to condemn oneself. Relative truth allows

---

[28] Art Lindsley. *True Truth: Defending Absolute Truth in a Relativistic World* (Kindle Locations 197-199). Kindle Edition.

humanity to choose when to use its version of Truth, where this version of Truth is to be dispensed, and what definition of Truth it will use for the situation at hand. This self-creation of relative truth becomes a confusing smorgasbord of lies smothered in the sweet cream of an amoral society. Therefore, its indecision of absolutes becomes its ultimate decision that God does not exist and therefore absolute Truth does not exist. Self-worship becomes the new worldview. If humanity becomes the judge of what is true and what is not, it will believe that all claims and beliefs are equally true. The result is the disintegration of Truth and what you have left are LIES. So, if we leave the definition of truth to humanity, which is imperfect, amoral, and mortal, one can be certain that Truth will not be absolute. Thus, the new politically correct "truth police" will judge Christianity to be just one of many truth"s" in the world.

In the book *"The Gagging of God"* D.A. Carson describes why for Christianity there can be no other alternative than to be Christologically exclusive. He says,

In the past, God spoke: He has always
been a talking God. But in these last days
the eschatological framework is inescap-
able. His final "Word" as it were, is His
Son, Jesus Christ. If this is true, to ignore
Him or treat Him as one option among
many is to defy God our maker and judge.
And one day we shall gave an account to
Him. If it is not true, then there is no value
in claiming Christian allegiance at all. The
whole is a sham, not one among many. In
the light of such texts, there is no third
option.[29]

Thus, if John Hick is correct in saying that the Gospel
of Jesus Christ is not the absolute Truth, then Truth will
never be found, because God does not exist. In this state,
to exist in a world without God would be to live in a

[29] D.A Carson *"The Gagging of God"* (Zondervan, Grand Rapids, Michigan,
1996), Pg. 345.

world of lies, and humanity would exist in self-servi-tude. Without the existence of God /Truth, humanity would be gods and would do what is right in its own eyes. Therefore the further we are from a relationship with God through Jesus, the less Truth will exist in our day-to-day lives. In fact, our choice to live life apart from God results in an entire worldview governed by lies, because there exists no partial truths.

A society governed by the absence of Truth (lies) will quickly become chaotic and result in a totalitarian gov-ernment. Society will have to resort to the law of "might is right" in order to sustain some form of civility. When society has abandoned God it also has abandoned a stan-dard or basis for absolute Truth. If there is no absolute standard for individual or societal behavior, the defini-tion of Truth will be lost, and there will be no need for the rule of law.

The teaching of absolute Truth must exist in order for humanity's structure of the law to have any effect. So far, much of our law has its fundamentals based on

the existence of God's biblical absolutes. When one testifies as a witness, he is asked to swear to "tell the Truth,
the whole Truth and nothing but the Truth." This oath
is a statement that the Truth is to be absolute, not relative. If the judge was to make his/her decision based on
a so-called "relative truth," no one would ever discover
absolute Truth. I do not know anyone who would want
the judge to decide that everyone is in some way guilty
and some way innocent. If we were falsely accused of
stealing, we would want the judge to discover the absolute Truth that we were innocent of the crime. Therefore
I conclude that if the law were based on relative truth,
there would be nothing left to judge.

Next I would like to take a brief look at the effects
that relativism has had on the foundation of Christianity.
I propose that if in fact Jesus is Truth personified, then
His death on the cross for all the sins of humanity is par-
amount to our salvation. As the dangerous ideology of
relative truth pervades our society, the need for the cross

and all it represents will slowly fade away until the death of Christ becomes meaningless.

DISINTEGRATION OF THE CROSS

Once the devil was walking along with one of his cohorts. They saw a man ahead of them pick up something shiny. "What did he find?" asked the cohort. "A piece of the truth," the Devil replied. "Doesn't it bother you that he found a piece of the truth?" asked the cohort. "No," said the devil, "I will see to it that he makes a religion out of it."[30] I believe that the devil is pleased any time humanity discovers "a piece of truth" because this takes their eyes off Jesus as the absolute Truth. He knows that even a small representation of Truth is still a lie because it is not pure. Pluralism (truth with an "s") has become a religion with many pieces of truth totally destroying the need for the final work that Jesus did on

---

[30] Klyne Snodgrass, *Between Two Truths - Living with Biblical Tensions,* 1990, Zondervan Publishing House, p. 35.

the cross as the payment for forgiveness of sins on behalf of all humanity. As the Truth of the cross slowly erodes, the necessity of the forgiveness of sins is moot, and our only hope is based on good works. If good works are the basis for our salvation, then Christianity is on par with all other religions, and the death of Christ was meaningless. If Jesus did not have to die for all the world's sins, the cross disintegrates, and Christianity as a whole is useless because humanity is still dead in its sins. In 1 Corinthians 15:12-20 the apostle Paul describes that without the death of Jesus on the cross and His subsequent resurrection three days later, Christianity has no merit.

"But tell me this—since we preach that Christ rose from the dead, why are some of you saying there will be no resurrection of the dead? For if there is no resurrection of the dead, then Christ has not been raised either. And if Christ has not been raised, then all our preaching is useless, and your faith is useless. And we apostles would all be lying about God—for we have said that God raised Christ from the grave. But that can't be true if there is no resurrection of the dead. And if there is no resurrection of the dead, then Christ has not been raised. And if Christ has not been raised, then your faith is useless and you are still guilty of your sins. In that case, all who have died believing in Christ are lost! And if our hope in Christ is only for this life, we are more to be pitied than anyone in the world.

But in fact, Christ has been raised from the dead. He is the first of a great harvest of all who have died."

Hick presupposes that traditional Christianity's faith in Jesus as the embodiment of Truth is irrational and thus lacks warranted belief. Yet, since it has been ascertained that everyone has faith in something, how can one know which faith is the one which is a rational and thus warranted Truth? Is the Christian community rational and thus warranted in its belief, or is there reason to assume that this doctrine is epistemically unacceptable, as Hick would imply?

According to Plantinga, if the traditional Christian belief is true it also has warrant, and warrant is "intimately connected with proper function. More fully, a belief has warrant just if it is produced by cognitive processes or faculties that are functioning properly,"[31] according to how humanity was designed to function. This line of reasoning would show that there is no sign from the historical accounts given in the New Testament that any cognitive processes of Jesus were not functioning properly. His behavior (words, actions, beliefs) was logically coherent, reasonable, and backed by convincing evidence. It would also appear that those following Jesus as apostles or as His disciples also had all their created faculties functioning properly, and there is no evidence that their memory was fading or that their minds had any mental deficiencies. Consequently, there would be more than sufficient warrant to believe that the Christ-events His followers had experienced and passed on to the

---

[31] Alvin Plantinga, *Warranted Christian Belief* (Oxford: Oxford University Press, 2000), xi.

church were epistemically, historically, metaphysically, and theologically the Truth. Thus, it is highly plausible that Jesus' words in the New Testament and in particular John's Gospel are trustworthy and True. On the other hand, if they are proven not to be trustworthy and True, the cross of Christ must fade into oblivion, because it is then a lie. If it is a lie, then it cannot be placed alongside thousands of many truth "s." The meaning of the cross slowly disintegrates.

TRADITIONAL CHRISTIAN

I have chosen to use the term "traditional Christian" to refer to adherents of the Christian faith who affirm the historical teachings and doctrines of the church about Jesus Christ as "Truth" which has been passed on and defended for two thousand years. I also affirm Bloesch and his centrist evangelical theology, which holds to "the sense of reclaiming the dynamic center of Biblical and apostolic faith of God's self-revelation in Jesus Christ."[32] Bloesch claims that this type of traditional Christianity does not accept everything in its "tradition uncritically. It is alert to what the Spirit of God is doing in the culture without trying to accommodate the claims of the gospel to cultural ideologies."[33] A traditional Christian, according to Oden and Packer, is one who believes the Bible to be the Word of God and views the "cross as the place where salvation was won, conversion as a universal need and missionary outreach as a universal task."[34]

ABSOLUTISM/EXCLUSIVITY/PARTICULARISM

I have heard some argue that to make absolute truth claims of any one religion is arrogant. And yet, I would say that those who deny absolutes are the ones that are arrogant. "Relativism arrogantly maintains that there

---

[32] Donald Bloesch, *Jesus Christ: Savior and Lord* (Downers Grover: Inter-Varsity Press, 1997), 11.

[33] Ibid., 11.

[34] J. I. Packer and Thomas C. Oden, *One Faith: The Evangelical Consensus* (*Downers Grove:* Inter-Varsity Press 2004), 19.

are absolutely no absolutes. On the other hand, absolutes can be asserted without arrogance."[35] Used in the
context of traditional Christianity, the term "absolute,"
"exclusive," or "particular" would say that for one to say
that God revealed Himself in the flesh to humanity
through Jesus Christ and that only through Him can
human beings find forgiveness of their sins and be saved
may be done without arrogance. Saying that Christianity
is True all the time, for everyone, everywhere is reality.
I would argue that having an arrogant faith is in itself, a
contradiction because one's true faith in Christ should
birth humility, not arrogance. Therefore it is possible to
believe that Jesus is the absolute Truth for the entire world
and still not be arrogant. If I were to state that gravity is
an absolute law of physics, would that statement be arrogant? Yet Lindsley warns us that, "Knowledge can lead
to humility or arrogance. It is possible, though not easy,

---

[35] Art Lindsley. *True Truth: Defending Absolute Truth in a Relativistic World*
(Kindle Locations 385-386). Kindle Edition.

to keep our balance, asserting the truth we have discovered as a result of God's grace without being arrogant."[36]

Here is a good example of how absolute Truth works. Imagine that Bob walks into a room and notices three people sitting on a sofa. Bob asks the question, "What is the temperature in here?" The first person shakes and exclaims, "It's freezing in here!" The second person casually said, "I'm fine, it isn't cold in here." The third person was much more animated and jumped off the sofa and and yelled, "It is so hot in here I can't stand it!" "The temperature in the room was affecting them in different ways, but it does not change the fact that the temperature of the room was 70 degrees. Truth may affect people different ways. An absolute truth itself can not be different than what it actually is."[37] "D'Costa describes the exclusive paradigm as holding to the belief that "other religions are marked by humankind's fundamental sinfulness and are therefore erroneous, and that Christ (or

---

[36] Ibid, 425-426.
[37] Confident Christians, *http://www.confidentchristians.org/six_steps_resources/Does%20Absolute%20Truth%20Exist.pdf* Copyright © 2007.

Christianity) offers the only valid path to salvation."[38] Nash describes exclusivism as having two propositions: "(1) Jesus Christ is the only Savior. (2) No one can be saved unless he or she knows the information about Jesus' personal work contained in the Gospel and unless he or she exercises explicit faith in Jesus Christ."[39] The Truth is the Truth and therefore must be particular, especially when it exists in the form of a living Deity, namely Jesus Christ. According to Netland, an exclusivist believes that "God has revealed himself definitively in the Bible and that Jesus Christ is the unique incarnation of God, the only Lord and Savior. Salvation is not to be found in the structure of other traditions."[40]

Hick's denial of Jesus Christ as the living Truth and incarnation of God is not a new challenge to Christianity; in fact, it has become a common theme

---

[38] Gavin D'Costa, *Theology and Religious Pluralism: The Challenge of Other Religions* (Oxford: Basil Blackwell Ltd., 1986), 52.

[39] Ronald Nash, *Is Jesus the Only Savior?* (Grand Rapids: Zondervan Publishing House, 1994), 25.

[40] Harold Netland, *Dissonant Voices: Religious Pluralism and the Question of Truth* (Grand Rapids: Eerdmans, 1991), 9.

within most modern theologies. Hick has stated that if the incarnation is literal, then God has revealed Himself exclusively through Jesus Christ. In his discussion, Bloesch refers to Brunner, who called exclusivity the scandal of particularity. This "scandal" is the "fact that God became a man at one point in history, that God revealed Himself among one particular people in history, that God revealed Himself in this people, and in this person is definitive and final."[41] These assertions of the Truth have led to accusations of traditional Christianity being an insular or narrow-minded religion; however, in reality, exclusivists believe that the gospel Truth of Jesus is open to the entire world.

I believe that traditional Christians must emphasize "the scandal of *universality*: that this one salvation is intended for all, that Christ's salvation goes out to all, including the outsider and the sinner."[42] From this perspective, Jesus Christ is the only True standard by

---

[41] Donald Bloesch, *Jesus Christ: Savior and Lord* (Downers Grover: Inter-Varsity Press, 1997), 237.
[42] Ibid., 236-7.

which every religion, and especially Christianity, must be understood and tested. Schenk asserts, "Exclusivists insist that Christ is unique, final, decisive, and normative as the self-revelation of God, for the salvation of the world."[43] Jesus is not only the greatest God in the midst of other gods, but according to Shenk, "There can be no other Lord besides Him. This exclusive claim is not a footnote to the gospel. It is the gospel."[44]

---

[43] Calvin E. Shenk, *Who Do You Say That I Am? Christians Encounter Other Religions* (Scottdale: Herald Press, 1997), 34.

[44] Ibid., 35.

CHAPTER TWO

WHY JOHN HICK?

"Hick's misguided views of God's revelation as Truth and his unwillingness to accept the absolute authority of Scripture are at the root of his theological diversion, eventually leading him to the creation of his pluralistic hypothesis (truth with an 's')." - Author

INFLUENCES OF
JOHN H. HICK

John Harwood Hick was born in
January 1922 to Mark and Aileen Hick
in Scarborough, England...In 2011 the
University of Birmingham launched
the John Hick Centre for Philosophy of
Religion and later the same year awarded
him an honorary doctorate of divinity, at
which time he gave his last public speech.
John Hick died on February 9, 2012,
just weeks after celebrating his ninetieth
birthday.[45]

---

[45] David Cramer, *Internet Encyclopedia of Philosophy*, http://www.iep.utm.
edu/hick/, Accessed March 8, 2017.

have chosen to respond to John Hick's brand of pluralism primarily because he has articulated in philosophical terms the thoughts and beliefs of Western postmodern, post/truth society. In Netland's opinion, Hick is seen as "one of the most influential philosophers of religion and theologians of the twentieth century [who] has since the late 1970s, been an indefatigable apologist for pluralism."[46] He is the appropriate figure to examine in this book, because he claims to have had a Christian conversion experience, and then soon after abandoned his short lived faith.

HICK'S FUNDAMENTALIST EXPERIENCE

Hick explained that he would go to church services with his grandma in Hull England, and one day when he was 12 years old he experienced a powerful evangelical

---

[46] Harold Netland, *Encountering Religious Pluralism: The Challenge to Christian Faith and Mission* (Downers Grove: Inter-Varsity Press, 2001), 158.

conversion to fundamentalist Christianity.[47] He states
that he "entered with great joy and excitement into the
world of Christian faith ... [and] ... accepted as a whole
and without question the entire evangelical package of
theology."[48] Hick shared that one day his grandmother
invited the well-known Welsh evangelist, George Jeffreys
into her house for a party. Jeffreys was a powerful char-
ismatic preacher who founded the Four Square Gospel
Alliance. Hick recalls that after the guests left, there was
a prayer meeting in Granny's dining room and the children were included. He said, "I was kneeling at a chair
when Jeffreys, coming round the circle, laid his hands on
my head. I immediately felt a strong physical effect, like
an electric shock except that it was not a sharp jolt but a
pervasive sensation spreading down through my body. I

---

[47] John Hick, *An Autobiography*, Oneworld Plublications, (185 Banbury Road, Oxford OX2 7AR, England, 2002), 27.

[48] John Hick, *"A Pluralist View"* in Dennis L. Okholm and Timothy R. Phillips (eds.), *Four Views: Salvation in a Pluralistic World* (Grand Rapids: Zondervan Publishing House, 1996), 30.

was in floods of tears –not of sadness or fright but I suppose, a tremendous emotional impact."[49]

There is no doubt that something did happen that day to the young Hick and that at one time he did for a brief time believe that Jesus Christ is God and the only way to salvation. Yet, I wonder what happened to change the faith of this young man from the traditional Christian worldview of exclusivity? We may never know, and yet there is some evidence that a true conversion may never have occurred. In my research I noticed that each time Hick shared his conversion experience there was no reference made to repentance, and a decision to have Jesus become Lord of his life. I cannot be sure that this necessary action did not occur in his life; however it is absent from his accounts. The Scriptures are clear that where there is no repentance, there is no salvation. (2 Corinthians 7:9-10) explains, "Yet now I am happy, not because you were made sorry, but because

---

[49] John Hick, *An Autobiography*, Oneworld Plublications, (185 Banbury Road, Oxford OX2 7AR, England, 2002), 27&28.

your sorrow led you to repentance. For you became sorrowful as God intended and so were not harmed in any way by us. Godly sorrow brings repentance that leads to salvation and leaves no regret, but worldly sorrow brings death." Regarding his past Christian experience, Hick shares from his Hull students' journal, "Reading all this now I see how my intellectual development has been surprisingly consistent apart from the interruption of the evangelical years.... I believed absolutely in some sort of divine reality, though not the God of Christian orthodoxy. Clearly I was in a religiously questioning and open state."[50]

Later, Hick believed he was attracted more by theosophy (collections of mystical and occultist philosophies) than the Christianity with which he was familiar. He confesses, "after a while I consciously dismissed it, with its precise levels of existence and invisible spheres and ranks of angelic beings, as too neat and tidy and professing to know too much. What I gained from it

---

[50] Ibid, 33.

however was an interest, which continued until my evangelical Christian conversion and then hibernated for many years, in the eastern religions."[51] My thought would be, that if Christianity had all the answers and was so neat and tidy that maybe this is so because it is the Truth. Interestingly, Hick describes his mother Aileen as being psychic herself, and at times would play the Ouija board with her friends. He admits to becoming very curious regarding the paranormal and procured professional mediums in London for several séances. Hick became a member of the S.P.R. (Society for Psychical Research) for many years. He was encouraged to be involved by his Oxford doctoral supervisor, H. H. Price, whom he praises as "one of the most highly intelligent people I have known, and author not only of important books on epistemology but also of fascinating philosophical discussions of psychical research, or parapsychology as it is known today."[52]

---

[51] Ibid, 31.
[52] Ibid, 29.

After World War II, Hick returned to his studies in philosophy at Edinburgh University and continued his association with the Evangelical Union. However, he felt as if he no longer fit in. In time, he began to have many doubts about his traditional evangelical faith. Later he became a critic of evangelical theology, because as he explains, " I saw it as a form of doctrinal (and sometimes also biblical) fundamentalism, with all the dangers of the fundamentalist mind-set, I can nevertheless genuinely understand the evangelicals' point of view, having once fully shared it for several years."[53] He felt that traditional Christianity provided few answers to his questions about apparent contradictions in the Scripture and conflicts between science and the Bible. Hick claims that in 1961 his "first departure [from conservatism] occurred [when he] questioned whether belief in the Incarnation required one to believe in the literal historicity of the Virgin Birth."[54]

---

[53] Ibid, 35.
[54] Ibid, 32.

Today, as one reads from his voluminous books on pluralism and Christianity, it is obvious that Wilfred Cantwell Smith, a Yale professor and a former evangelical missionary to India who also converted to pluralism, profoundly influenced Hick. Philosophically, Hick was strongly influenced by philosopher Emmanuel Kant and his "Epistemological Model." Gavin D'Costa, a well-known critic of Hick, suggests that one can see a Kantian perspective throughout Hick's work. The influence of Kant, he says "can be seen as the ambiguous archetype of latter-day pluralism, [which he believes is] the term given to those who hold that all religions are revelatory and therefore capable of being means to salvation, and that this salvation is not causally, ontologically, or historically related to Jesus Christ."[55]

Because of his unique background in traditional Christianity, Hick comes to this debate with a fair understanding of traditional exclusivist beliefs. It is the

---

[55] Gavin D'Costa, "Revelation and World Religions" in Paul Avis, (ed.), *Divine Revelation* (Grand Rapids: W. B. Eerdmans Publishing Company, 1997), 120-1.

author's assertion that Hick's misguided views of God's revelation could have been as a result of his early exposure to the occult and his unwillingness to accept the absolute Truth of Scripture. Whatever happened, Hick's theological diversion eventually led him to the creation of his pluralistic hypothesis (Truth with an "s").

Hick's beliefs are more fully developed in his book *An Interpretation of Religion,* where he explains his pluralistic hypothesis in detail. He affirms that in the light of a new and greater understanding of various world religions, all claims and dogmas of exclusive traditional Christianity must be abandoned in order to accept the "Ultimate Real." He argues that as Christianity abandons its claim of exclusive religious superiority, it will pass a perilous point and enter a "new territory from which the whole terrain of Christian truth is bound to look different."[56] Ultimately, Hick is asking those who hold to traditional Christianity to abandon the exclusive doc-

---

[56] John Hick, "The Non-Absolutism of Christianity" in John Hick and Paul F. Knitter (eds.), *The Myth of Christian Uniqueness* (New York: Orbis Books, 1987), 22.

trines it has affirmed for over 2000 years and in so doing, add an "s" to the Truth and adopt a new contradictory understanding of who God is.

Today's Western world is increasingly prepared to throw Truth away and to embrace this new pluralistic ideology; in fact, more of the church has been affected than one might imagine. It is this threat to one's faith in Jesus Christ, the disintegration of the cross, abandonment of Truth, and the only hope for the salvation of this world that has impassioned me to write this book.

IDEOLOGICAL PLURALISM AND THE DISINTEGRATION OF TRUTH

While the world has always been pluralistic, we are currently experiencing a kind of pluralistic revival never before seen in the history of humanity. Pluralism has come to mean more than the Western world's acceptance of multiple faiths in a multicultural society. Today's pluralism has developed a new ideological character of its own, denying Jesus as the personification of the Truth and resulting in the slow disintegration of His salvific work on the cross. Catholic theologian Walter Cardinal Kasper believes that this situation "calls Christianity fundamentally into question and ... challenges the church in an entirely new way."[57] He explains that because of globalization, contemporary human beings are forced to live out their national and personal lives in many different worlds at once. The result, according to Kasper, "is a patchwork identity, a syncretistic tapestry of interchangeable pieces drawn from the most disparate religious and cultural traditions."[58] Within this patchwork, few people have a clear enough understanding to be able to pick out what is true or false; the result is a weakened society full of open seams and fractures. Postmodern philosophy has desperately attempted to hold the seams together and discover new ways to heal the fractures. In

---

[57] Walter Cardinal Kasper, "The Uniqueness and Universality of Jesus Christ" in Massimo Serretti (ed.) *The Uniqueness and Universality of Jesus Christ: In Dialogue with the Religions* (Grand Rapids: Ecrdmans Publishing Company, 2004), 7.

[58] Ibid.

this process, society has concluded that there is only one way to unify the world, by embracing "a new qualitative pluralism in which there are no longer any absolute values and norms. Reason has become plural in itself. Truth, humanity, and justice exist only in the plural."[59]

Consequently, no definition of absolute Truth remains, nor is there any desire to arrive at such a definition because they have denied the very God in whom the Truth resides. This vacuum leaves society no choice but to create a new tolerance and freedom that perceives all belief systems, including non-religious ideologies, as equally valid and as containing truth "s" relative to the environment in which they were fostered (relativism). Pluralists believe it is no longer possible to have universal and objective Truth because of the assumption that "God or the Absolute reveals itself under innumerable names all of which are true."[60]

---

[59] Ibid.
[60] Ibid., x.

Since contemporary society has no desire to engage the Christian church about the question of who the Truth is, in its absence, the criteria left for separating core religious beliefs from non-core beliefs disintegrate. This leaves no need to discover the difference between authentic beliefs and false superstitions, true experience from illusion, myth from fact, or the reasonable from the absurd. Ultimately though, as in any discussion regarding God, one's "understanding of Jesus depends fundamentally upon what [one] believe [s] about God."[61] For example, it shall be made clear, as one understands Hick's hypothesis, that his view of God's nature and being is radically different from that of the traditional Christian view. Geivett states, "What we believe about God and His relationship to the world sets the conditions for what is both psychologically possible and rationally permissible for us to believe about

---

[61] Douglas R.Geivett, *"Is Jesus the Only Way?"* in Michael J. Wilkins and J. P. Moreland (eds.), *Jesus Under Fire* (Grand Rapids: Zondervan Publishing House, 1995), 179.

Jesus."[62] Therefore, one can assume that the question surrounding Jesus' deity and His unique incarnation is also a question about God and revelation. A plain denial and faulty understanding of God as Truth and of how He revealed Himself to humanity can ultimately lead to a faulty understanding of who Jesus actually was and is. Karl Barth said, "In the doctrine of God we have to learn to say God in the correct sense. If we do not speak rightly of this subject, how can we speak rightly of His predicates?"[63]

DANGER OF REDEFNING GOD'S SELF-REVELATION AS THE TRUTH

A holistic understanding of God's self-revelation as the Truth is vital to the doctrine of the incarnation and the exclusivity of Jesus. I will argue that Hick's redefinition of the traditional Christian belief in God's

---

[62] Ibid., 160.
[63] Karl Barth, *Church Dogmatics,* translated by T. H. L. Parker et al., ed. G. W. Bromiley and T. F. Torrance (Edinburg: T. & T. Clark, 1957), 2 (1): 3.

self-revelation as the Truth has led to his denial of other major doctrines. Hick's ideology of God's self-revelation to humanity has affinities with the eastern concept of an impersonal and polytheistic unknowable "Real." According to Hick, God "is always and everywhere present to us above, beneath, around, and within us. And when a human being is exceptionally open to the divine presence, he or she has a vivid awareness of God, which is then called revelation."[64] This definition sounds very open and tolerant; however, it is so loose that God is reduced to whatever one's "vivid awareness" imagines Him to be.

Donald Bloesch defines the traditional meaning of revelation as "the movement of God into a particular human history, that is, the personal history of Jesus Christ and the self-communication of God to His people both through events surrounding Jesus Christ and through the inspired witness to these events which

---

[64] Hick, John, "A Pluralist View" *in* Dennis L. Okholm and Timothy R Phillips (eds.), *Four Views: Salvation in a Pluralistic World* (Grand Rapids: Zondervan Publishing House, 1996), 34.

together constitute the Holy Scripture."[65] Although it seems logical that God would interact with humanity by personally revealing Himself to them, nonetheless human beings continue to explain the existence of God through their own philosophies, using abstract concepts of being. Bloesch says in *God the Almighty* that Barth "broke with his tradition by contending that we really know the hidden God in his self-revelation in Jesus Christ. What God is in himself is identical to what He is in the revelation in Christ."[66] Archie Spencer, professor of Theology at Trinity Western University, claims that Christianity is unique because it believes in the revelation of God to humanity.

He contends, however, that today "revelation has become merely the historical confirmation of what man

[65] Donald Bloesch, *Jesus Christ Savior and Lord* (Downers Grove: Inter-Varsity Press, 1997), 239.

[66] Donald Bloesch, *God the Almighty: Power, Wisdom, Holiness, Love* (Dowers Grove: Inter-Varsity Press, 1995), 32.

can know about himself and therefore about God apart from revelation."[67]

Michael Green explains that there are only two revelatory religions in the world in which God has revealed Himself on a personal basis - "Only Judaism and its "child" Christianity maintain that God has given a reliable and personal disclosure of Himself [as the Truth] to human kind."[68]

As mentioned earlier, the Western world has incorporated the lie of "new" pluralism into the very heart of its culture and has denied the meaning of Truth by denying the self-revelation of God as Truth.

---

[67] Archie Spencer, "The Pluralist and Inclusivist Appeal to the Religious Sense as a Basis for Inter Religious Dialogue" in Appendix 2, *God the Creator, Sustainer and Redeemer,* (Short Notes for Students, summer, 2005), 18.

[68] Michael Green, *But Don't All Religions Lead to God?* (Grand Rapids: Baker Books, 2002), 27.

CHAPTER THREE

JOHN HICK'S TRUTH 'S' HYPOTHESIS

"It is important for the reader to
understand that Hick's ideology did
not suddenly appear in a mature and
fully developed form. It did not grow
smoothly, but developed "fitfully" over
time as Hick tried one theory after
another in order to make his evolving
view of pluralism work."- Ronald Nash

HUMANITIES CONTINUING PROCESS IN THE DISCOVERY OF TRUTH 'S'

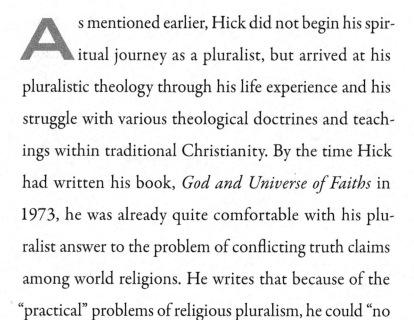

As mentioned earlier, Hick did not begin his spiritual journey as a pluralist, but arrived at his pluralistic theology through his life experience and his struggle with various theological doctrines and teachings within traditional Christianity. By the time Hick had written his book, *God and Universe of Faiths* in 1973, he was already quite comfortable with his pluralist answer to the problem of conflicting truth claims among world religions. He writes that because of the "practical" problems of religious pluralism, he could "no longer find it possible to proceed as a Christian theologian, as though Christianity was the only religion in the world."[69] In the remainder of this book, he lays out his understanding of a Christian theology of religions. What Hick has essentially done is to totally deny God's own revelation through the incarnation of Jesus Christ as the embodiment of Truth itself and has embraced an ideology of the devil's lie disguised as Truth with an "s".

Hick has totally rejected any theology that restricts itself to a particular religion specific to a culture. He observes that the older traditional view of Christian theology should not be viewed as the divine revelation of God/Truth but rather as a "body of divinely revealed truths."[70] On the other hand, Hick envisions his "new" theology for modern humanity as "a continuing process of human reflection and theorizing that aims to clarify the meaning of man's religious experience."[71] His goal is

---

[69] John Hick, *God and the Universe of Faiths* (London: Macmillan Press Ltd., 1973), 132.
[70] Ibid., 104.
[71] Ibid.

to create a new definition of contemporary theology, the working out of a global theology of religions.

Hick was strongly influenced by the Oxford movement. In *The Myth of God Incarnate* he refers to his involvement in the movement as a revolution of sorts. However, Catholic theologian, Karl-Heinz Menke has observed that the ideas in the book were revolutionary only to those "who had failed to see the drift of the Oxford incarnation Christology toward a 'Spirit Christology'"[72] In addition to Cantwell Smith, another theologian greatly admired by Hick was Perry Schmidt-Leukel, who successfully brought Hick's Gradualistic Christology into the "arena of German academic theology."[73] Menke observes that Hick "merely brings the

[72] Menke, Karl-Heinz, *"Jesus Christ: The Absolute in History?* The Question Concerning the Universal Significance of a Historical Fact" in Massimo Serretti (ed.), *The Uniqueness and Universality of Jesus Christ* (Grand Rapids: Eerdmans Publishing Company, 2001), 135. "Spirit Christology" denies any Trinitarian foundation within Christology. Menke explains that "Lampe relativizes the hypostasis of the Son by calling it a projection of the historical Jesus and his relationship to the Father into the essence of God." 136. For more information read, Geoffrey W. Lampe's "Spirit-Christology" (God as Spirit: The Bampron Lectures, 1976 [Oxford, 1977]).
[73] Ibid.

ideas of the Oxfordian Spirit Christology to a sharper point insofar as he attempts to dialogue with analytical philosophy and accommodates the self understanding of non-Christian religions."[74]

Nash believes that it is important for the reader to know that Hick's ideology "did not suddenly appear in a mature and fully developed form."[75] He explains that it did not grow smoothly, but developed "fitfully" over time as Hick tried one theory after another in order to "make his evolving view of pluralism work."[76] Nash believes that Hick's present pluralistic hypothesis evolved naturally to include a wider array of religious and secular belief systems. As his theory began to change over time, it also became necessary for Hick to abandon some of his old ideas and add new concepts to his hypothesis as critics observed flaws and contradictions. Nash divides

[74] Ibid., 138.
[75] Ronald Nash, *Is Jesus the Only Savior?* (Grand Rapids: Zondervan Publishing House, 1994), 29.
[76] Ibid., 30.

Hick's primary changes into two stages the first stage develops the need for the second.

STAGE #1: HICK'S COPERNICAN REVOLUTION.

Philosophically, Hick's hypothesis was strongly influenced by Immanuel Kant's "Epistemological Model" which became a vital component of what Hick has called his "Copernican Revolution." In the 1970s, John Hick believed that his theories about world religions were so radical and revolutionary that he decided to describe his approach as a Copernican Revolution. Around CE 100 to 170, an astronomer and mathematician by the name of Claudius Ptolemy lived in Alexandria, Egypt, and taught that the sun and all the planets revolved around the earth. Nicolas Copernicus (CE 1473-1543) later challenged this belief, asserting that the earth and all the planets revolved around the sun, which was the center of the planetary system. Since then, it has been quite

common for scholars "who have a dramatically new idea
to propose to describe it as a 'Copernican Revolution.' "[77]
Hick, however, uses the term metaphorically to compare
what he considers to be the old, outdated Christocentric
exclusivist method of an absolute revelation of God
(Ptolemaic model) with the new postmodern pluralistic
understanding of world religions that is centered on one
Theocentric God (Copernican Model). Hick begins the
explanation of his new revolution with a question, "Do
we regard the Christian way as the only way, so that salvation is not to be found outside it; or do we regard the
other great religions of mankind as other ways of life
and salvation?"[78] The hard reality of what traditional
Christian exclusivity really meant so haunted Hick that
he began to question God's love for *all* humanity. He
could not understand, if God really desired to see all
humanity come into His kingdom, why then "must men
be saved in such a way that only a small minority can

---

[77] Ibid.
[78] John Hick, *The God and the Universe of Faiths* (London: The Macmillan Press Ltd., 1973), 121.

in fact receive salvation."[79] Hick abandoned Truth and chose to believe that many modern Christian thinkers have abandoned traditional Christianity and are seeking other alternatives to understanding the human condition because of this moral contradiction.

The historical church has, according to Hick, been deeply entrenched in a dogma of exclusivity that refuses to allow for any salvation outside of the church. Pope Boniface VIII proclaimed this traditional position in 1302. However, Hick believes that since then humanity has gained a greater understanding of the Truth with an "s" inherent within all world religions. Consequently, asserts Hick, the Catholic Church has been in the process of changing its views and has admitted that "such a dogma, as it was understood in the medieval church, is unattainable . . .."[80] However, even this slow disintegration of the essential Truth of the cross which has led to a progress towards pluralism has not given Hick much

---

[79] Ibid., 122-3. Ibid., 123.
[80] Ibid., 123.

comfort, since he believes that the church continues to add what he calls "epicycles" to bolster this dying dogma of the deity of Jesus as the Truth and the exclusivity of the Christian faith.

According to Hick, an "epicycle" is a theory created to change a foundational dogma without verbally altering it. He used this metaphor "because they [Christocentric dogmas] are so powerfully reminiscent of the epicycles that were added to the old Ptolemaic picture of the universe, with the earth at the center, to accommodate increasingly accurate knowledge of the planets."[81] This ancient model asserted that the stars, planets, and even the sun orbited around the earth. However, it was eventually discovered that while the stars seemed to be moving in that mode, the planets and the sun actually moved in ways that did not fit that theory. Hick explains that rather than discarding the old theory, "the ancient astronomers added a series of smaller supplementary circles, called epicycles, revolving with their centers on

[81] Ibid., 124.

the original circles."[82] Finally, some astronomers realized that Copernicus had made the mistake of using circles to describe the rotation of the planets. Only after Johannes Kepler was able to clearly explain that the planetary orbits are elliptical and not circular was the Copernican theory accepted as fact."[83] Nash explains that Ptolemaic astronomers continually attempted to create additional epicycles in order to prolong the life of the old model; however, over time the process was becoming too complex. The Copernican theory was eventually accepted because of its simple way of explaining the difficult and complex orbits of the planets. Copernicus began a revolution in astronomy that literally changed forever the way human beings would view the universe and their part in it. The earth's human occupants had always thought of themselves as being at the center of everything, but now they had to accept that they were only a small part of something much bigger. This new realization that the

[82] Ibid., 125.
[83] Ronald Nash, *Is Jesus the Only Savior?* (Grand Rapids: Zondervan Publishing House, 1994), 31-2.

sun rather than the earth was at the center meant that humanity inhabited only one of many planets revolving around one common star; this paradigm shift opened the way to many other changes in society.

Hick strongly believes that, just as the Copernican revolution radically transformed humanity's view of the universe, an equally radical transformation must occur in Christian theology. He asserts that his theory is the simplest hypothesis accounting for all the world's major religions and their variant forms. Each individual religion, he believes, must come to view itself as only one of many faiths, all revolving around the same "Reality." This revolution "involves a shift from the dogmatic belief that Christianity is at the center to the realization that it is God who is at the center, and that all the religions of mankind, including our own, serve and revolve around Him."[84] This theory, which Hick calls the "Copernican Revolution" in theology, has become his primary

---

[84] John Hick, *God and the Universe of Faiths* (London: Macmillan Press Ltd., 1973), 130-1.

justification for rejecting traditional Christianity's exclusive doctrine of the incarnation of Jesus as Truth. Yet as we shall see, there are a number of major flaws in Hicks comparison between the scientific error that the Ptolemaic astronomers made to God's declaration of being the personification of Truth without an "s."

It is clear in Hick's book, *God and the Universe of Faiths* that he views anyone disagreeing with his new theological revolution as antiquated. He boldly proclaims that this outdated Ptolemaic label must be applied to "any view that places Christianity at the center of the world's religions."[85] Thus, any attempts by exclusivists to defend the position that Jesus is God or that Christianity is the only true faith must be viewed as narrow-minded and intolerant. According to Hick, Christian exclusivists are prime examples of the fabricated, capricious, and counterfeit measures of religious Ptolemaic epicycles. He does admit however, that Christianity is not alone

---

[85] Ronald Nash, *Is Jesus the Only Savior?* (Grand Rapids: Zondervan Publishing House, 1994), 32.

in its "dogmatic" claim: all religions have their Ptolemaic views or tendencies because they have not yet seen his "truth," that there are many truth"s." Hick says that all one must do to discover truth"s" is to "stand back from the arena of competing systems, surveying the scene as a whole in order to see what is hidden from the Ptolemaic believer."[86] These old and narrow views, asserts Hick, are usually dependent on the cultural context of the Ptolemaic believer; this biased environment cannot possibly be a reliable source of Truth. Yet the real source of Truth does not come from an earthly enviroment it comes from the God who exists as the Truth alone. Hick attempts to use a personal example to explain, "I myself used to hold to a Ptolemaic Christian theology; but if I had been born to a devout Hindu family in India . . . I should probably have held a Ptolemaic Hindu theology instead."[87] He concludes that it is possible to preserve one's own Ptolemaic view, "but when we are conscious

---

[86] John Hick, *God and the Universe of Faiths* (London: Macmillan Press Ltd., 1973), 132.
[87] Ibid.

of its historical relativity we may feel the need for a more sophisticated, comprehensive and globally valid theory."[88] It becomes more and more evident as one reads Hick's flawed understanding of truth"s" that even if one is born into a belief system which is based on a lie, this understanding will be believed and even passed on until God/Truth is revealed. There are many examples of children born into cults and dangerous ideological belief systems that continue to follow the evil ways of their parents. Yet being born into a false worldview does not excuse one of hearing and following Truth. Romans 1:18-21 clearly states,

> God shows his anger from heaven against all sinful, wicked people who push the [truth] away from themselves. For the [truth] about God is known to them instinctively. God has put this knowledge in their hearts. From the time the

---

[88] Ibid.

world was created, people have seen the earth and sky and all that God made. They can clearly see his invisible qualities his eternal power and divine nature. So they have no excuse whatsoever for not knowing God. Yes, they knew God, but they wouldn't worship him as God or even give him thanks. And they began to think up foolish ideas of what God was like. The result was that their minds became dark and confused" (NLT)

According to Hick, the only way that those advocating a Ptolemaic faith of Christian exclusivity can accept his "new" Copernican revolution is by not being firm in their commitment to their theology. The person not entrenched in the original dogma of his faith will, he says, discover "the resulting picture of artificial, implausible, and unconvincing, and ... be ready for a Copernican revolution in his theology of religions."[89]

---

[89] Ibid., 125.

In this early development, Hick describes God as an "infinite divine reality that exceeds all human thought,"[90] but later he suggests that God is unknowable. In creating a concept of God as unknowable, Hick is removing personality from his understanding of God, enabling him to incorporate all postaxial religions into his hypothesis. This change signals the beginning of the second stage of Hick's hypothesis in which he adds essential elements to strengthen his theory. Hick needed a second stage in his pluralistic development that could include the major eastern religions he had excluded from his first stage.

STAGE #2: THEOCENTRIC TO SALVATION-CENTERED THEOLOGY

Kant's epistemological model became the foundation for Hick to begin moving away from his God-centered model to his concept of an "unknown entity"

---

[90] John Hick, *God and the Universe of Faiths* (London: Macmillan Press Ltd., 1973), 178.

that is neither personal nor impersonal. Hick needed a definition of God that could incorporate both Eastern and Western concepts of God and yet still maintain a common element of salvation/liberation.

While Hick was in graduate school at Edinburgh University, he began to incorporate the philosophical insights of Immanuel Kant. As his hypothesis continued to develop, Hick discovered Kant's epistemological model with its theories of knowledge, and he adapted them to fit his particular model. Nash finds it significant that Kant "had described his own theory of knowledge as a Copernican Revolution in philosophy. Kant's 'revolution' attacked the usual way philosophers had thought about human knowledge before he came along."[91] Prior to Kant's revolution, philosophers had placed reality at the center of epistemological methodology [the knowing method]. As a result, all knowledge was believed to proceed directly from reality; however,

[91] Ronald Nash, *Is Jesus the Only Savior?* (Grand Rapids: Zondervan Publishing House, 1994), 39.

Kant believed that there was much more to knowing. He proposed an idea conceived earlier by Thomas Aquinas, who stated, "Things known are in the knower according to the mode of the knower."[92] In other words, Aquinas was saying that someone or something else might perceive one person's experience of something in the real differently. Hick explains, "The human mind is not a passive screen on which the world imprints itself. On the contrary, it is continuously involved in interpreting the data of perception in terms of the conceptual systems in which we live."[93] This epistemological principle of Kant claims that what one observes in the world is only a part of what is reality, because that particular perception of reality comes from one individual. Kant realized that what humanity knew of the world was dependent on two details, the "information received through the

---

[92] Thomas Aquinas, *Summa Theologica*, II/II, Q.1, art.2.

[93] Hick, John, "A Pluralist View," in Okholm, Dennis L. Phillips Timothy R. (eds.) *Four Views: Salvation in a Pluralistic World* (Grand Rapids: Zondervan Publishing House, 1996), 46.

senses and the organizing powers of the human mind."[94] Nash observes that this new concept of the way human beings view their world "required Kant to distinguish between the way the world appears to us (the phenomenal world) and the way the world really is (the noumenal world)."[95] If the way the world looks to us is not the way the world really is, there must then be another world behind what we see - a noumenal world. Thus, says Hick, "We must distinguish between the world as it is in itself, unperceived, and that same world as humanly perceived."[96] An example would be a microbe perceiving in its world what a human mind could never perceive. Likewise, a Buddhist born in Tibet would perceive the "Ultimate Reality" through a completely different lens than a Christian from America; however, the object perceived has not changed. Hick asserts, "We therefore have

---

[94] Ronald Nash, *Is Jesus the Only Savior?* (Grand Rapids: Zondervan Publishing House, 1994), 40.

[95] Ibid.

[96] Hick, John, "A Pluralist View," in Okholm, Dennis L. Phillips Timothy R. (eds.) *Four Views: Salvation in a Pluralistic World* (Grand Rapids: Zondervan Publishing House, 1996), 46.

to distinguish, as Immanuel Kant did, between a thing as it is in itself and that thing as humanly perceived, that is, as phenomenon."[97]

HICK'S PERCEPTION OF GOD BEGINS TO CHANGE

Hick took a strand of Kantian thought and added it to his own epistemology of religion; this addition resulted in a major change in the way he perceived God. Nash observes that "basic to Hick's move to a second stage of pluralism is his distinction between the phenomenal God and the noumenal God."[98] Thus, this distinction enables Hick to explain how the many differing world faiths perceive God or the same reality from completely different perspectives. He explains that "the 'Ultimate Reality' is known in accordance with the cognitive mode/nature/state of the knower; and this varies, in

---

[97] Ibid., 46-7.
[98] Ronald Nash, *Is Jesus the Only Savior?* (Grand Rapids: Zondervan Publishing House, 1994), 41.

the case of religious awareness, from one religiocultural totality to another."[99] According to Nash, what Hick is implying is that "all of the phenomenal concepts of God we encounter in the religions of the world are misleading, and inadequate. What we should be seeking is god as it, he, or she is in itself."[100] Then, once the "Real" is perceived as noumenal (unknowable reality), one will be able to see "how there is a plurality of religious traditions constituting different, but apparently more or less equally salvific, human responses to the Ultimate. These are the great world faiths."[101] Thus we must ask the question; Who or what is this unknowable "Ultimate Real?" In no time at all Hicks has managed to disintegrate the person of God as the embodiment of Truth and has reduced Him into a cosmic force of some kind

[99] Hick, John, "A Pluralist View," in Okholm, Dennis L. Phillips Timothy R. (eds.) *Four Views: Salvation in a Pluralistic World.* (Grand Rapids: Zondervan Publishing House, 1996), 47.

[100] Ronald Nash, *Is Jesus the Only Savior?* (Grand Rapids: Zondervan Publishing House, 1994) 41.

[101] Hick, John, "A Pluralist View," in Okholm, Dennis L. Phillips Timothy R. (eds.) *Four Views: Salvation in a Pluralistic World* (Grand Rapids: Zondervan Publishing House, 1996), 47.

of thing, or an it. Hick now brings us full circle to the question once again, is there one God/Truth or are there Truth"s"?

THE UNKNOWABLE "REALITY"

Within the second stage of Hick's pluralistic development, it becomes painfully obvious that he has switched from belief in a God who is both personal and impersonal to a noumenal perception of an unknowable Ultimate Being or energy force. Nash criticizes Hick as making a puzzling attempt to cover the mistakes of his first stage, wherein he has articulated a more "theistic, even Christian concept of God."[102] Hick declares that every religious belief system that has developed within the great post-axial religions of history, including Christianity, is a provisory response within a specific culture to the "Ultimate Reality" (the "Real"). Within the

---

[102] Ronald Nash, *Is Jesus the Only Savior?* (Grand Rapids: Zondervan Publishing House, 1994), 41.

first few chapters of his book, he attempts to quickly eliminate the old concept of "God," since it conjures up too many Western images of personhood. The word that Hick prefers to use for his more eastern perception of God is the "Real," "Reality," or the "Ultimate Reality." Hick defines his preferred description of the "Ultimate Real" thus,

> "that punitive reality which transcends everything other than itself but is not transcended by anything other than itself. The Ultimate, so conceived, is related to the universe as its ground or creator, and to us human beings, as conscious parts of the universe as the source of both of our existence and of the value or meaning of that existence."[103]

---

[103] John Hick, *Disputed Questions in Theology and the Philosophy of Religion* (New Haven: Yale University Press, 1993), 164.

Timothy O'Connor explains that when we come into contact with the "Real," "our minds actively (though unconsciously) process it in a way that that makes it understandable to us."[104] Thus, a Christian experiences the "Real" as the Heavenly Father, Son, and Holy Spirit (Trinity), while a Zen Buddhist experiences the "Real" as Satori, a Muslim as Allah, and a Sikh as a Satguru. In the Hindu religion, this perception of the "Real" is manifested as Vishnu, along with a multitude of gods and goddesses, including Krishna and Rama (incarnations of Vishnu) and Shiva. Hick claims that all these millions of gods within Hinduism, no matter how different they may be, are still "seen as manifestations of the ultimate reality of Brahman."[105] Yet he believes "all these communities agree that there can ultimately be only one God!"[106] Followers of Islam, Christianity, and Judaism

---

[104] O'Connor, Timothy, "Religious Pluralism" in Michael Murray (ed.), *Reason for the Hope Within* (Grand Rapids: William B. Eerdmans Publishing Company, 1999), 176.

[105] John Hick, *Disputed Questions in Theology and the Philosophy of Religion* (New Haven: Yale University Press, 1993), 38.

[106] Ibid.

believe in a God of substance and personality; however, faiths such as Hinduism and other eastern sects believe in an impersonal "Ultimate Reality." Hick states that neither of these perceptions is accurate because "it" is "one of many, active or passive, substance or process, good or evil, just or unjust, purposive or purposeless." [107] In Hick's view, one cannot apply categories or a character of any kind to the "Real" because classifications are human concepts related to human experience; therefore, there is no way of knowing whether the "Ultimate Real" is good or evil.

Hick explains that each tradition acts as a mental lens consisting of religious concepts "stories (both historical and mythical), religious practices, artistic styles, forms of life through which we perceive the divine."[108] Since there is a great plurality of these "lenses" in the world, one may experience and think of the "Real" in a plurality of ways. Hick defends the belief that the "Ultimate Reality"

---

[107] John Hick, "The Theology of Pluralism," *Theology 86* (1993): 337.
[108] John Hick, *Disputed Questions in Theology and the Philosophy of Religion* (New Haven: Yale University Press, 1993), 159

is unknowable; next to his concept of the Copernican Revolution of religion, this premise is the lifeblood of his pluralistic hypothesis. It is interesting to note here that Hick has added an "s" to the word Truth and yet his argument for plurality also implies that the "Ultimate Real" is quite absolute.

This added concept of the unknowable "Reality" is very important to Hick's rejection of exclusivity and the deity of Jesus Christ. First, if Hick's Copernican Revolution is correct and "god" or the Ultimate Real is at the center of the religious world and is found within all the great post-axial religions, Christianity can no longer remain Christocentric. Second, if Jesus is no longer at the center of Christianity, then the Christian claims of God's revelatory plan to save the world through the incarnation of Christ are also false. Thirdly, if God as Father, Son, and Holy Spirit are one of many so called Truth"s" then the logical conclusion would be that the God of the Bible is not the embodiment of Truth and is in fact a lie. Finally, the Christian community can no longer believe that Jesus is the personification of the Way, the Truth, and the Life, or that He is divine, or that He historically rose from the dead. If God is neither personal nor impersonal, reduced to an unknowable "it" (noumenal), then the concept of humanity having a personal relationship with God through Christ is not possible, and Jesus becomes only one spiritual representative among many. Thus, according to Hick, Christianity is no longer warranted to believe that God revealed Himself to the world exclusively through the incarnation of Jesus Christ and is thus one more lie among many lies. From this perspective, Jesus, Mohammed, Buddha, Krishna, and the Jewish prophets are all equally representative human manifestations of the Ultimate Real; however, none of them can actually be the "Real/Truth." According to Hick, the primary goal for every religion, especially Christianity, is to begin to understand the Ultimate Real as being at the center of the religious universe and to embrace a new theology of religions that includes all faiths.[109]

---

[109] Ibid., 160-2.

However, to make way for this new theology, Christianity must shed nearly everything that defines Christians as Christ followers, leaving very little of the original Christian faith intact. According to Hick, the list of old theologies Christians must shed includes all the doctrines essential to traditional Christianity. From a traditional Christian perspective, the following list of theologies and doctrines that must be eliminated in order to accept Hick's "new" theology is staggering:

1. Any of the divine revealed truths such as the Trinity and the two natures of Jesus;

2. The creation of the world by His spoken word;

3. The fall of humanity and is continued depravity from birth;

4. That God came to humanity through the incarnation of Jesus to die for the sins of the world and provide forgiveness to all who come to Him in faith;

5. The virgin birth of Jesus;

6. The miracles of Jesus involving any disruption from the natural order;

7. That Jesus' physical body rose from the dead, returned to life and was seen in person by many eye witnesses;

8. That the only way to salvation for all humanity is to respond to God's call on their life through Jesus;

9. At the point of death an individual's relationship within God cannot be reversed;

10. Heaven and hell are literal places.[110]

What is left of the original Christian faith? Surely no more than a few wise sayings uttered by a delusional Jewish teacher who was not any closer at His death to revealing the unknowable "Reality" than He was before He came to earth.

Hick affirms that the doctrine of the incarnation, "instead of continuing to be regarded as sacrosanct,

---

[110] John Hick, *God and the Universe of Faiths* (London: Macmillan Press Ltd., 1973), 92-3.

should be openly reconsidered."[111] Yet, why should it be "reconsidered" if there is cognitive warrant for believing it to be true? Hick's own belief in this unknowable Reality is not warranted simply because this Reality cannot be known in a cognitive way. He can only explain what the Real is not and that Truth is not singular. As Stetson states, "It would seem that negative prediction, to be informative, must have some positive knowledge of its subject; there must be some pre-existent, known truth about the subject."[112] If one does not know anything about an object, then the object will have no meaning unless by its very existence it can be shown to have certain characteristics. Hick seems to avoid the subject of existence and thus reveals that his explanation of the unknowable qualities of the Real *an sich* as noumenon/phenomenon cannot cognitively be understood. Stetson believes that Hick is an agnostic pluralist because of his

---

[111] John Hick, *The Metaphor of God Incarnate*, (Louisville: John Knox Press, 1993), 2.

[112] Brad Stetson, *Pluralism and Particularity in Religious Belief* (Westport: CT Preger Publishers, 1994), 7.

faith in the "Unknowable Real," "yet Hick seems to be able to describe the "it" as quite knowable in his book *An Interpretation of Religion.*"[113] Hick describes what the Real is not with some detail and even claims that "it" is neither "good nor evil." Nash points out that "once it becomes clear that we all lack awareness of whether the Real is good or evil, who can say that an evil cult may not function as an authentic response to the Ultimate?"[114] Stetson claims that if "God or the Real actually were absolutely unknowable, then we should not know that it is loving and morally disapproving of Soteriological exclusivism."[115] He continues to say that the "most we could ever be epistemically justified in saying about the divine and its essential intentions and purposes is that we know nothing about them."[116] Thus, it would be more rational to believe in the light of so many conflicting and

---

[113] Ibid.

[114] Ronald Nash, *Is Jesus the Only Savior?* (Grand Rapids: Zondervan Publishing House, 1994), 43.

[115] Brad Stetson, *Pluralism and Particularity in Religious Belief* (Westport: C.T. Preger Publishers, 1994), 23

[116] Ibid.

incompatible truth claims that there is no Truth at all rather than to believe Hick's hypothesis that all claims are equally True. Thus, if there is no Truth there is no God, which is illogical, because the spark of life exists and motion is continuous.

The problem is that Hick's pluralistic hypothesis was created in the womb of philosophy, which is the only place an ideology constructed from weak epistemological theories can safely exist and survive. God's Word warns, "See to it that no one takes you captive through philosophy and empty deception, according to the tradition of men, according to the elementary principles of the world, rather than according to Christ" (Colossians 2:8). As pluralism has become an ideology and moved into the real world, it has not been able to sustain itself; it is in essence self-destructing, because pluralism cannot be true to itself and be simultaneously exclusive. Those who attempt to truly live out Hick's philosophical pluralism fail, because the ideology cannot be lived out in the real world. According to Montgomery, "General philosophical skepticism is a nice intellectual game, but one cannot live by it."[117]

What Hick reveals at the close of his second stage is that his move from belief in a personal God to a perception of an impersonal unknowable Ultimate Reality clouds his theory's relationship to any human experience. Hick's god or "it" may be quite compatible with some eastern religions; however, in choosing to create a non-being that is "neuter," he has managed to erase all personality from his concept of God. In doing so, he ostracizes the two major axial of religions such as Judaism, and Christianity that believe in a personal and relational God.

---

[117] John Warwick Montgomery. *The Shape of the Past* (Ann Arbor: Edwards Brothers, 1962), 140.

A GRADING STANDARD FOR WORLD RELIGIONS (SALVATION/LIBERATION)

In Hick's book, *An Interpretation of Religion,* he appears to confirm his belief that all religions are equal; however, as one takes a closer look, it becomes evident that he has very particular standards by which he grades religions. A brief examination of Hick's version of the development of religious history sheds light on why he believes that each faith must abandon its particular archaic theology for a "new theology" of world religions. The old theology, according to Hick, "has been developed within the confines of a particular confessional conviction which construes all other traditions in its own terms."[118] An example would be traditional Christian theologies that claim God's self-revelation to humanity came in the form of a Trinity - Father, Son, and Holy Spirit, three persons

---

[118] John Hick, *An Interpretation of Religion: Human Responses to the Transcendent* (New Haven: Yale University Press, 1989), 1.

but one in essence. These theologies assert that God came in the flesh through the exclusive incarnation of Jesus, and that all other religions are constructs of human merit. It says in John 14:6 and Colossians 1:15, "[Jesus] is the image of the invisible God, the first born over all creation." In traditional Christian theology, salvation is available to all humanity through the economic work of Jesus on the cross; humanity is saved through faith in Jesus and by the grace of God (Titus 2:11). In contrast, Islam claims that there is no other god but Allah and that there could never be a division of god into human form. "We shall not serve anyone but Allah, and we shall associate none with Him" (Koran 3.64). Salvation in Islamic theology depends on accepting Allah's guidance to direct one's actions and attitudes (Koran 17.13).

These individual differences of theology within religions must be accounted for, says Hick, and this can be done only by moving beyond the "dominant self understanding of each tradition."[119] He contends that over time

---

[119] Ibid., 2.

each faith comes to believe that its particular theology is exclusive of or superior to the other world faiths and thus cannot accept any notion of salvation outside of its own theological boundaries. Hick's solution is an authentically pluralistic hypothesis that will ultimately call for or "at least be [an] implication for further development within each of the traditions."[120] Hick believes that this "new theology" would theoretically account for the "data and theories of the human sciences" by showing how "the response to a transcendent reality has taken the bewildering plurality of forms that history records."[121]

Hick's particular view of religion centers on a natural religion, a "religion without revelation." In other words, humanity has a type of religious instinct that is built into its anthropological character. The Eternal One, according to Hick, has applied very little pressure of His presence upon the human mind. Hick believes that to observe the difference between "natural religion" and the "great world

---

[120] Ibid.
[121] Ibid.

faiths," we must be willing to perceive the Ultimate Real workingwithin the complete religious life of humanity, "challenging men in their state of 'natural religion,' with all its crudities and cruelties, by the tremendous revelatory moments which lie at the basis of the great world faiths."[122] Gregory H. Carruthers explains that to Hick the great world religions "all have God's free revelation at their center as the cause of their existence."[123]

Hick advocates a "new theology of world religion" in *An Introduction of Religion* and loosely divides the progress of human religious faith into three basic ages. First was the pre-axial age that existed from pre-historic time to 800 BCE and was an age of religious appeasement to the gods. Second, was the axial age which lasted from 800-200 BCE and centered mostly on religious individuality. Finally, today's post-axial age, during which humanity has

---

[122] John Hick, *God and the Universe of Faiths* (London: The Macmillan Press Ltd., 1973), 180.

[123] Gregory H. Carruthers, S.J., *The Uniqueness of Jesus Christ in the Theocentric Model of the Christian Theology of World Religions: An Elaboration and Evaluation of the Position of John Hick* (Lanham: University Press of America, 1990), 39.

evolved to a higher state of worship, has lasted from 200 BCE to the present. Hick believes that humanity's religious evolution was a gradual process, similar to the gradually developing scientific understanding of man's macro development from protein to homosapiens. As humanity grew in understanding, they developed a primitive understanding of worship and gradually developed a more advanced need for salvation/liberation in all world religions.[124] Thus, Hick concludes that the "generic concept of salvation/liberation, which takes a different specific form in each of the great traditions, is that of the transformation of human existence from self-centeredness to Reality-centeredness."[125]

Hick regards his approach to world religions as the appropriate Christian theology for today because, in his view, theology is a constantly changing and growing organism. He admits that his use of the term "different faiths" refers primarily to the great world religions;

---

[124] John Hick, *An Interpretation of Religion: Human Responses to the Transcendent* (London: The Macmillan Press Ltd, 1989), 21-69.
[125] Ibid., 36.

however, he leaves open the possibility for a broader acceptance of faiths into his fold. He clarifies that his terminology does not imply that "other smaller and other newer religions, as well as 'primal' religion, and the great secular faiths of Humanism and Marxism, are not in themselves of equal intrinsic importance. ..."[126]

His development of a "new" interpretation of religion has enabled Hick to formulate a new pluralistic theology of religion that can broadly yet effectively unify all world faiths and belief systems exhibiting a form of salvation/liberation. Thus, Hick is now able to include even secular belief systems such as Communism and Humanism in his pluralistic circle.

Having established scientific and religious theories of the historical evolution of world faiths, Hick is able to attack the individual religious theologies that are, in his view, self-centered and exclusive. By examining his "new" understanding of theology, one is able to see why Hick

---

[126] John Hick, *The Rainbow of Faiths, A Christian Theology of Religions* (Louisville: John Knox Press, 1995), 11.

would reject traditional Christianity's claim that God is the personification of the Truth; in his eyes, this claim is implausible. According to Hick, "There has not been a singular revelation, but a plural one ... no one religion can claim to be the true religion. For a true relationship to God may occur in each of the great religions."[127] Yet how is one able to have a "relationship" with an unknowable, beingless, force of energy? Thus Hick contends that the doctrine of the incarnation of Jesus in one specific thread of human history such as Christianity should not be viewed as the only saving economy. In fact, Hick strongly believes that Jesus never claimed His own deity, and secondly that the deity attributed to Him in history happened over a graduated process. Therefore in chapter four I would like to observe Hick's two major objections as to Jesus' being the Truth personified.

---

[127] Gregory H. Carruthers, S.J., *The Uniqueness of Jesus Christ in the Theocentric Model of the Christian Theology of World Religions: An Elaboration and Evaluation of the Position of John Hick* (Lanham: University Press of America, 1990), 41

CHAPTER FOUR

JOHN HICK'S OBJECTIONS

1. Jesus never claimed his own deity: (Personification of Truth = God).

2 The deification of Jesus was a historical process.

> "This apparent evidence of process theology has convinced Hick and like-minded thinkers that over time the church developed humanly constructed theologies like the incarnation to create an exclusive religion of dominating power." - Author

JOHN HICK'S TWO PRIMARY OBJECTIONS

H ick's hypothesis lays the foundation for his rejection of the exclusive doctrine of the deity of Jesus Christ. Thus, his objections will reflect why he believes that he is justified to "reexamine" and therefore expel the doctrine of Jesus' incarnation and any other resulting Christocentric theology. Essentially, Hick rejects all and any passages in the Holy Scriptures where Jesus reveals Himself as Truth personified. He asserts that "at the end of the twentieth century Christianity is in a deep crisis. The theological structure developed by the Western church has come to seem hollow and irrelevant to the majority of Westerners."[128] In this light, providing an adequate response to his hypothesis becomes even more pressing; however, his primary objections to Jesus' deity must first be clearly understood.

From a traditional Christian perspective, the cause of this "crisis" is the pluralist decentralizing of Christ, the only Truth, the source of all power and authority of the church. If one removes the lifeblood (Christ) from this organism, it will become "irrelevant" to its followers because it will become "hollow" and dead. John Hick is one of many twentieth century writers responsible for the slow but sure disintegration of the Cross of Christ and its salvic power for a sinful and confused world. The church has believed for two millennia that the forgiveness of humanity's sin comes through faith in the only One who can remove that sin and change lives (Jesus the Truth). Hick, on the other hand, believes this contemporary crisis is due to the church's stubborn desire to hang

---

[128] John Hick, *The Rainbow of Faiths: A Christian Theology of Religions* (Louisville: Westminster John Knox Press, 1995), ix.

on to old worn-out Christocentric doctrines rejected long ago by many of its members. He would likely define this crisis as the culminating struggle of the church's coming of age in a postmodern world of many faiths, as it attempts to free itself from the bondage of its antiquated Ptolemaic theology of epicycles. Hick believes that his "Copernican revolution" in the theology of religions challenges all faiths to turn their attention to a salvation/liberation model of an unknowable "Ultimate Reality." Yet if this were true, Christianity would no longer exist and would in some way be swallowed up by an Eastern religious entity of confusion, worshipping a noumenal (non personal) "it" or energy force. Since Hick's primary objections take aim at the deity of Jesus as Truth, discussion of them will therefore include some references to this central doctrine. My intent is not to downplay the importance of Hick's other objections; however, Hick's rejection of the incarnation doctrine (which pre-supposes deity) is pivotal to the success of his hypothesis. Hick raises two specific but interconnected primary objections to the deity of Jesus:

1. **Jesus never claimed His own deity (Truth Personified).**
2. **The deification (incarnation) of Jesus was a created historical process.**

Hick's main argument, based on these two primary objections, is that traditional Christianity does not have sufficient warrant to continue believing in the self revelation of God through the exclusive incarnation of Jesus Christ. If, as Hick asserts, Jesus never claimed to be God, then the logical status of the incarnation doctrine would be moot because it presupposes that Jesus was self-conscious of His own deity and was the Truth.

OBJECTION #1: JESUS NEVER CLAIMED HIS OWN DEITY

Hick's basis for rejecting this doctrine is what he views as solid evidence that the self-claim passages and all Biblical references to Jesus as Truth personified and exclusivity were developed by Christian writers. Thus, he feels justified in eliminating most of John's gospel, the Pauline epistles, along with any other passages in the Bible that allude to Jesus' claim to deity.

Hick strongly believes that in recent times there has been a major movement of Christian philosophers, theologians, and Christian church leaders towards his new pluralistic theology of religions. He argues that this change has been gradually occurring for nearly two hundred years, predominantly among the mainline churches (liberal theology) that "have allowed their theologies to develop in line with the new knowledge."[129] Hick's term

---

[129] John Hick, *The Metaphor of God Incarnate*, (Louisville: John Knox Press, 1993), 7.

"new knowledge" refers to a more informed understanding that the historical Jesus did not believe He was divine nor that He was the only way of salvation. He claims that since the prophecy of the second coming did not occur as His disciples had thought, "Jesus was gradually elevated within the Gentile church to a divine status."[130] Discrediting the doctrine of the incarnation is so vital to Hick that he published a book called *The Metaphor of God Incarnate* in which he establishes his interpretation of a non-literal incarnation. Traditional Christianity has consistently taught and believed that Jesus was the literal incarnation of God and that He not only knew He was God but proved it by His actions on the earth. Hick reasons that if Jesus did not teach that He was God incarnate, then the church must have developed this doctrine shortly after His death, culminating at the Council of

---

[130] Ibid., 4

Nicaea in CE 325.[131] This doctrine, is according to Hick, "a creation of the church, one that Jesus himself would probably have regarded as blasphemous." [132]

Hick asserts that fundamentalists simply settle any debate about the incarnation by quoting the self-claim passages of Jesus from John's gospel, for example, "I am the way, the truth and the life ..." (John 14:6) Hick believes this response is mainly due to the ignorance among fundamentalists created by their church leaders and to their lack of desire to ask the difficult questions about their problematic theology (incarnation/exclusivity).[133] One of the difficult questions the church is avoiding, according to Hick, is why Jesus did not directly

---

[131] Hick believes that the doctrines of high Christology, such as the Incarnation, and the Trinity were fully adopted by the church at the Council of Nicaea convened by Constantine in 325 CE. The main purpose was to heal a schism in the church induced by Arianism. For more information regarding Nicaea see: Walter A. Elwell, (ed.), *Evangelical Dictionary of Theology* (Grand Rapids: Baker Book House, 1984), 774-6. For John Hick's point of view see John Hick, *The Metaphor of God Incarnate* (Louisville: Westminster/ John Knox Press, 1993), 44-5.

[132] Hick, John, "A Pluralist View" in Dennis L. Okholm and Timothy R. Phillips, (eds.), *More Than One Way: Four Views on Salvation in a Pluralistic World* (Grand Rapids: Zondervan Publishing House, 1995), 52.

[133] Ibid.

say that He was God incarnate, consubstantiated with the Father. The problem with this argument is that I do not know of any pastor in any evangelical church that would avoid the question of Jesus' deity or the fact that He is the only way of salvation. To the contrary, evangelical pastors preach on the subject regularly, because they know that if Jesus is not the Truth personified, there is no hope for humanity to be reconciled with God, and they might as well stay home (as the Apostle Paul would say).

Hick concedes that one cannot make any statements of certainty about what Jesus actually thought about Himself; however, he asserts that the existing evidence has led historians studying that period of history to conclude that Jesus did not claim deity. My question would be that if one cannot make any claims of certainty, then how can one make any conclusions about anything, including pluralism. Hick quotes from Michael Ramsey, James Dunn (out of context), C.F.D. Moule, and Brian Hebblethwaite, claiming that all of them agree that Jesus never claimed deity.[134] However, what Hick does not acknowledge in his discussion is that most of these historians do accept Jesus' self-consciousness about who He was, evidence clearly implying that Jesus was aware of His deity throughout His ministry. Hick, however, simply chooses to ignore the larger context for the statements of these authors. For example, while Dunn refers to the fact that Jesus does not come right out and claim to be God consubstantiated with the Father and the Holy Spirit, Dunn does acknowledge that Jesus was completely conscious of His own divinity and revealed it in many other ways. In his book *The Evidence for Jesus,* Dunn affirms his belief and confidence "in the God and Father of our Lord Jesus Christ."[135] However, despite these discrepancies, Hick still quotes these authors, forcing their words to suit his own purposes.

---

[134] John Hick, *The Metaphor of God Incarnate* (Louisville: John Knox Press, 1993), 27.

[135] James Dunn, *The Evidence for Jesus* (Philadelphia: The Westminster Press, 1985), 107.

Hick claims that scholars have been asserting increasingly that Jesus did not claim His divinity and that this "reflects a remarkable transformation resulting from the modern historicocritical study of the New Testament."[136] Yet, there has been virtually no change or "transformation" in the traditional Christian understanding that Jesus is God. Rather, it is the old liberal guard that has distorted what was upheld as truth by the historical Christian church for over two thousand years. Hick believes that the reason why so many Christians still believe that Jesus Himself claimed His literal incarnation is due to ignorance "usually undisturbed by their pastors [that] still makes it difficult for basic theological issues to be discussed in the church in an open and genuinely inquiring way."[137]

What about the Biblical evidence that Jesus forgave sins and thus held Himself above the Jewish law? Surely this evidence proves that He recognized his Deity. Hick's

---

[136] John Hick, *The Metaphor of God Incarnate* (Louisville: John Knox Press, 1993), 28.
[137] Ibid., 29.

response to this question is to ask whether Jesus really did "abrogate the Torah, and did He in fact do what only God can do in forgiving sinners?"[138] Why, I ask, would he even question whether or not Jesus forgave sinners as only God could do? The primary message in the First Covenant (OT) was a foreshadow of the fulfillment of Christ's coming in the Second Covenant (New Testament). All the feasts of the Tabernacle from the First Covenant reveal the Messiah's coming to forgive sinners, and the main point of the Second Covenant is to reveal the historical fact Jesus was the coming Messiah and that He would bring salvation for all humanity. From Matthew to Revelation the Good News expresses that the sins of the world can be forgiven through the death and resurrection of Jesus Christ/Truth. Yet knowing this, Hick still agrees with Sanders' explanation that Jesus never attributed to himself the authority that belonged to God, since "he only pronounced forgiveness, which

---

[138] Ibid., 28.

is not the prerogative of God, but of the priesthood."[139]
Then Hick concludes that "if one has already accepted a
form of orthodox Christology one can reasonably inter-
pret some of Jesus' words and actions, as presented by
the Gospel writers, as implicitly supporting that belief."[140]
In other words, he asserts that traditional Christianity
arrived at its particular belief that Jesus claimed His own
deity, and thus incarnation, because of a false theological bias.

For his final evidence that Jesus did not claim His
own deity, Hick borrows from an extremely liberal theologian named Rudolf Bultmann who uses the concept
called the "Christ-event." This "Christ-event," according
to Bultmann, "is supposed to consist not only in the life
of Jesus but also in the formation of the church and the
growth of its faith in Jesus' deity. It is the larger complex,
rather than Jesus' own words and actions, that are now

[139] E. P. Sanders, *Jesus and Judaism* (London: SCM Press, 1985), 240.
[140] John Hick, *The Metaphor of God Incarnate* (Louisville: John Knox Press, 1993), 33.

said to authorize the belief that he was God incarnate."[141]
Hick states, "In Bultmann's work, the use of the Christ-
event idea reflected a strong historical skepticism and a
consequent move from an ontological to an existential
understanding of Christ."[142]

Hick concludes that to affirm the incarnation "is thus
to affirm the church and the Christian story by which it
lives; and this does not require a prior or independent
judgment that the story is literally true."[143] Unfortunately,
making a statement such as, "Jesus never literally claimed
His own deity," and then building an entire theology
around it without substantial evidence does not make
it true. Both Hick's and Bultmann's arguments regarding
the deity of Jesus are in no way consistent with what we
see as the big picture of God's Word from beginning to
end. The entire Bible reveals that God is coming and has
come into the world to save humanity from the plague
of sin and will one day return again to restore a broken

[141] Ibid.
[142] Ibid., 35.
[143] Ibid., 36.

world. Remove that message and you will remove the reason it was written to begin with. Now let us move on to Hick's second objection to Jesus' being the personification of the Truth.

OBJECTION #2: HIGH CHRISTOLOGY: HISTORICAL EVOLUTION OF THE CHURCH

Hick explains how the man Jesus of Nazareth was transformed to become Jesus the God incarnated Savior of the world. Naturally, in his hypothesis, Hick rejects most of John's gospel and any other passage, that attributes even a hint of deification to Jesus. While Hick does not discard these passages of Scripture without giving reasons, he operates according to biased presuppositions. He believes that he is warranted to discard the Biblical passages because there is "enough" evidence (from Bultmann's use of the redaction method) that the biblical self-claim passages and references to Jesus' deity are not authentic. He claims that up to "about a hundred years ago (as still very widely today in unlearned circles) belief in Jesus as God incarnate was assumed to rest securely upon his own explicit teaching."[144] He maintains that most conservative (of which I don't see evidence) and liberal "mainline" scholars of the New Testament now agree that these "I Am" passages are not the actual words of Jesus; rather, they are the "words put into his mouth some sixty or seventy years later by a Christian writer expressing the theology that had developed in his part of the expanding church."[145] Hick claims that at the time of Jesus it was common for individuals to write speeches and attribute them to famous people, "embodying the writer's sense of the real significance of that past figure."[146] Therefore, he argues that the "discourses attributed to Jesus ("I am" passages) in the fourth gospel are seen today by most contemporary scholarships

---

[144] Hick, John, *"A Pluralist View"* in Okholm, Dennis L. Phillips Timothy R. (eds.) *Four Views: Salvation in a Pluralistic World* (Grand Rapids: Zondervan Publishing House, 1996) 53.

[145] Ibid.

[146] Ibid.

as examples of this."[147] According to Hick, none of the gospel writers were eyewitnesses to the events they were writing about some forty to seventy years after the fact. He contends that they merely wrote known stories about Jesus that had already been through a process of change and adaptation; thus, traditional Christianity must not view the gospels as historical documents. Hick states, "In the case of the 'I am' sayings I don't think any reputable scholar today would maintain that these words are of the historical Jesus."[148]

EARLY PROCESS OF THE DEIFCATION OF JESUS

Hick believes, the process of Jesus' deification occurred almost immediately after the death of this new religious leader. He contends that a transformation had occurred in those who encountered Jesus. To

---

[147] Ibid.

[148] John Hick, *The Rainbow of Faiths, A Christian Theology of Religions* (Louisville: John Knox Press, 1995),91.

the disciples, Jesus was "the center of their existence, the object of their devotion and loyalty...."[149] They began what Hick refers to as the early process of searching for words to describe their newfound master and Lord. Hick believes that the earliest teaching describing Jesus as more than a man had already begun with the words, "Jesus a Nazarene, a man attested to you by God" (Acts 2:22). Then thirty years later, Mark begins with the words, "In the beginning of the gospel of Jesus Christ, the Son of God . . ." (Mark 1:1). The process of deification then continued on for about another thirty years or so, as seen in John's gospel where "this Christian language is attributed to Jesus himself and he is depicted as walking the earth as a consciously divine being."[150] Hick contends that as the tight Christian community began to expand, most believers commonly referred to Jesus as their Lord; however, soon terminology that could more closely describe their understanding of the saving

---

[149] John Hick (ed.), *The Myth of God Incarnate* (London: S.C.M., 1979), 174.
[150] Ibid., 173.

power of Christ was required. This search for new titles for Jesus began first in the Jewish communities and then spread to the Gentile world within Rome. Hick argues that "these could only be the highest titles available ... the most exalted terms which their culture offered."[151] These titles began with the term "Messiah" and culminated with the term "incarnation." This process of additions is described by Hick as "that which began with Jesus as the Messiah of the Jews and culminated in the Nicene definition of him as God the Son, Second Person of the Trinity, incarnate."[152] We will discover in the next chapter Bultmann's theory of gradual high Christology has major flaws and does not reflect what we observe in the original texts. Nor does it reflect what we see in the words of the Creeds, in the words of the disciples' followers, in the words of historians of that time, or even in the words of the enemies of Christ themselves.

---

[151] Ibid.
[152] Ibid., 174.

In the *Myth of God Incarnate,* Hick concludes, based on his study of Gouler and Young, that ideas about divinity embodied in human life were quite widespread in ancient times.[153] Hick is adamant that the titles "Son of Man" and "the Messiah" were conferred upon Jesus by his disciples. He declares, "We know now that 'son of God' had long been a familiar metaphor within Judaism. Israel as a whole was God's son, Adam was God's son (Luke 3:28), the angels were sons of God (Luke 20:36), the ancient Hebrew kings were enthroned as 'sons of God,' hence the enthronement formula."[154]

Hick claims that in Judaism anyone close to God or having a special mission in life could be called a "son of God." He claims that the church created a unique meaning for this term by applying it solely to Jesus as the one and only Son of God. This exclusive meaning, argues Hick, emerged as the gospel was preached by the

[153] Ibid.

[154] John Hick, "What Does the Bible Really Say?" A sermon preached at Carrs Lane URC church Birmingham, July 2005. Available from http://www.johnhick.org.uk/; Internet; accessed, November 18th, 2005.

apostles in other parts of the world and finally in Rome. Under the leadership of Paul, the term "Son of God" was literalized and became part of the Christian doctrine. Then, "gradually in the course of the first centuries the metaphorical son of God was transformed into the metaphysical God the Son, second person in the divine Trinity."[155] Hick states it is easy to understand how Jesus, who came from the line of King David, could have metaphorically been called the "son of God."

The deification of Jesus, asserts Hick, may have begun with the title of Messiah; however, it culminated at the Council of Nicaea. Hick believes it was here that the Christian church exulted "the man of Nazareth into the divine Christ, the only-begotten of the Son of God, second person of the Holy Trinity."[156] This apparent evidence of process theology has convinced Hick and like-minded thinkers that over time the church developed

---

[155] Ibid.,168.
[156] Ibid.,169.

humanly constructed theologies like the incarnation to create an exclusive religion of dominating power.

In response to Hick's assertions, chapter five will show from historical affirmation that Jesus was seen as God/Truth within the immediate conception of the early Church. We shall see that large numbers of eye witness accounts can not be so easily dismissed. We will also examine background evidence from the early church, beginning with a look at specific passages of Scripture that clearly show a high Christology during the time of Jesus is present in all four gospels.

CHAPTER FIVE

HISTORICAL AFFIRMATIONS OF JESUS AS TRUTH

"The self-predicted resurrection of Jesus, observed by over five hundred eyewitnesses, only confirmed what the Christians already knew about Him, and the Holy Spirit sealed that knowledge within their hearts." - Author

AFFIRMATIONS OF JESUS' DEITY FROM SCRIPTURE

Richard Burridge and Graham Gould believe that the sources of high Christology, which see Jesus as "sharing the life of God, are there right at the earliest levels within the first communities of the Jewish believers, indeed perhaps even in Jesus' own self-understanding."[157] They claim that "this is not something that gets imported half a century later from a Greek background."[158] Words describing the divinity and exclusivity of Jesus Christ and the universality of the gospel are

---

[157] Richard Burridge and Graham Gould, *Jesus Now and Then* (Grand Rapids: William B. Eerdmans Publishing Company, 2004), 108.
[158] Ibid.

evident throughout the four gospels of Matthew, Mark, Luke, and especially in John.

Hick, however, denies the authenticity of passages supporting Christocentric theology that are found within the New Testament, mostly in John's gospel and Paul's letters. He argues that the "I Am" passages where Jesus claims His own divinity were "words put into his mouth some sixty or seventy years later"[159] by Christian writers expressing the theology that had been developed over time by the church.

My response to Hick's theories about the graduated deification of Jesus will reveal that history paints a very different picture than Hick has created. Historical documents demonstrate evidence of a very early deification of Jesus within the oral tradition (creeds), Paul's early letters of high Christology, testimonies articulating the early martyrs' worship of Jesus, and the Trinitarian language of the church fathers. It appears that early Jewish

---

[159] Hick, John, "A Pluralist View" in Dennis L. Okholm and Timothy R. Phillips (eds.) *Four Views: Salvation in a Pluralistic World* (Grand Rapids: Zondervan Publishing House, 1996), 53.

Christians believed Jesus was God incarnate long before the first gospel was penned because of His impact on their lives from the very beginning of His ministry. The prophetic and self-predicted resurrection of Jesus, observed by over 500 eyewitnesses, only confirmed what the Christians already knew about Him, and the Holy Spirit sealed that knowledge within their hearts.

PASSAGES IN JOHN'S GOSPEL AFFRMING JESUS' DEITY

To discover Truth, one must begin with a brief look at the main Biblical passages referring to Jesus' deity, exclusivity, worship, and incarnation; then one must test whether these passages confirm what was being said and practiced by Jesus' followers shortly after the events described in the gospels. As previously mentioned, Hick believes that credible modern scholars have deemed John's gospel as unreliable and as not penned by him. He claims that John could not have authored the book, because it is more theological than historical and because the deity passages ascribed to Jesus were added later. Yet, Hick offers mostly conjecture and created theories instead of solid evidence to back his statements. Let us look at some solid evidence to support John as the writer of the fourth gospel of Jesus Christ (Truth).

Theologian Craig Blomberg writes that complete commentaries and articles have appeared recently defending a considerable amount of the historicity of John's gospel; however, they have been ignored and remain virtually unchallenged by liberals. Blomberg mentions a few examples: "articles: Carson 1981b; E.E. Elis 1988; Sila 1988; Garcia-Moreno 1991; Baton 1993; Blomberg 1993; Lea 1995; Thompson 1996; D. Wenham 1997, 1998; de la Fuente 1998; Moloney 2000; commentaries: Bruse 1983; Michaels 1983; Beasley-Murray 1987; Carson 1991; Pryor 1992a; Morris 1995; Witherington 1995; Borchert 1996; Ridderbos 1997; Kostenberger 1999; Whitacre 1999."[160]

---

[160] Ibid., 21.

The book of John begins with a clear affirmation of Jesus' equality with God as the Truth through its use of the term "logos" or the living Word. Morris declares that there "was never a time when the Word was not. There never was a thing which did not depend on Him for its very existence."[161] The first verse of chapter one corresponds with Genesis, stating, "In the beginning was the Word, and the Word was with God, and the Word was God" (John 1:1). Thus, John immediately proclaims the pre-existence of Jesus, His divinity, and His involvement with creation. Gone are the days, argues Blomberg, "when scholars can plausibly argue that John's Christology must have been produced only at a very late stage of a slow, evolutionary development of Christian faith, removed from its Jewish roots within a dramatically different Greek milieu."[162] John 1:1 clearly

---

[161] Leon Morris, *The New International Commentary on the New Testament: The Gospel According to John* (Grand Rapids: William B. Eerdmans Publishing Company, 1989), 73.

[162] Craig Blomberg, *The Historical Reliability of John's Gospel: Issues and Commentary* (Downers Grove: Inter-Varsity Press, 2001), 25.

parallels Genesis 1:1, where the role of the Word is to be with God as well as to be God Himself.

Jesus claims to give humanity eternal life that no one can remove or steal. He says that God gave human beings to Him, and that there is no one greater than His Father; then, suddenly in the same breath, He boldly proclaims equality with God: "I and the Father are one" (John 10:28-30). John also describes the incarnation of Jesus as "the Word (who) became flesh, and dwelt among us, and we saw His glory, glory as of the only begotten from the Father, full of grace and truth" (John 1:14). John cites Jesus' claim to deity as the main reason the Jews wanted to kill Him. "For this reason therefore the Jews were seeking all the more to kill Him, because He not only was breaking the Sabbath, but also was calling God His own Father, making Himself equal with God" (John 5:18). After seeing and touching the wounds of the risen Jesus, Thomas calls Him "my Lord and my God" (John 20:28). No wonder Hick wants to desperately deny the veracity of John's gospel. It is full of verses which show that Jesus is God, the major theme from the beginning to the end.

John also depicts Jesus as the pre-existent incarnation of God, saying, "He was in the beginning with God" (John 1:2), and that He was not of this world (8:23). He states that Jesus had come from the Father (16:27) and would leave the world to go back to the Father (v 28). Jesus claimed to have existed before Abraham, using the term "I Am" that was reserved for God and was not used in common speech (8:58). Morris quotes C. G. Morgan, who believes the "I Am" saying of Jesus in this passage is a "supreme claim to deity . . . These are the words of the most impudent blasphemer that ever spoke, or the words of God incarnate."[163] Jesus also shared with the disciples that He would return to the glory He had before the world existed (John 17:5) and to the Father who loved Him before the foundation of the world (v 24).

---

[163] Leon Morris, *The New International Commentary on the New Testament: The Gospel According to John* (Grand Rapids: William B. Eerdmans Publishing Company, 1989), 73.

John also clarifies in his poetic style that Jesus is the exclusive Creator of everything that exists, "All things came into being through Him, and apart from Him nothing came into being that has come into being" (John 1:3). John makes obvious use of metaphor in order to show the purity of Jesus, comparing the light of his Holiness with the darkness that the world holds so dear. He concludes that the world will not recognize Him when He comes. "He came into the very world he created, but the world didn't recognize him. He came to his own people, and even they rejected him" (John 1:10-11). He pictures Jesus as the Light that came to shine before all men (John 1:9) and to take away the sin of the whole world (1:29). John describes God as having exclusively self-revealed Himself to humanity through Jesus, saying that eternal life can be found only by knowing "the only true God, and Jesus Christ whom [He has] sent" John 17:3. In the most famous "I Am" passage of (John 14:6), John clearly quotes Jesus as presenting Himself as the only avenue for the world's salvation. Here Jesus not only claims that He is the Way, the Truth, and the Life, but that He is also the exclusive representation of God incarnate, since no one can come to the Father without going through Him. Blomberg explains that, since Mark 1:2-3 declares John the Baptist would prepare the way of the Lord, "for the Messiah to come and claim to be that way proves merely to be the natural fulfillment of the prediction."[164] Blomberg also wonders whether the self-designation of the early church as "the Way" was based on this passage.[165] If his assertion is true, it offers additional evidence that the early church understood Jesus to be God/Truth and the only way to the Father. Thus, Hick's theory that the passages of Jesus' deity emerged from later developments in church theology can be seriously questioned. In John 3:16, Jesus declares that having faith in Him is the only way to achieve eternal life, since God gave to the world "His *only* begotten Son." Exclusivity is also apparent in verse 18, which ends with the sad reality that

---

[164] Craig Blomberg, *The Historical Reliability of John's Gospel: Issues and Commentary* (Downers Grove: Inter-Varsity Press, 2001), 198.
[165] Ibid.

all those who do not believe in Jesus will be condemned
(John 3:16-18).

The Jews wanted to have Jesus killed, not necessarily
because He claimed to be the king of the Jews or because
He cleared the Temple, but because He claimed to be
the "Son of God" (John 19:7). They tried a number of
times to have Him killed for claiming to be God (John
19:7; 10:36) and were eventually successful in bringing
about His death. It seems unlikely that the Jewish leaders
would have forgotten His previous claims to be the "I
Am" who was before Abraham was born (John 8:58).

Not surprisingly, Hick has a strong dislike for the
gospel of John because of its profusion of verses affirming
the deity of Jesus. As Nash asserts, "If Jesus really said
the things attributed to him in the fourth gospel, Hick's
efforts to attack the high Christology that grounds
exclusivism would be doomed."[166]

---

[166] Ronald Nash, *Is Jesus the Only Way?* (Grand Rapids: Zondervan Publishing
House, 1994), 84.

MATTHEW'S GOSPEL AFFRMS JESUS' DEITY

Passages referring to the exclusive divinity of Jesus are not found only in John but also in the book of Matthew. From the very beginning of Matthew the deity of Jesus is clearly emphasized, even in its account of His birth and the announcement of His name, "Emmanuel," meaning "God with us" (Matthew 1:21, 23). Matthew records that Jesus was worshiped by the Magi from the East (Matthew 2:11) and that the disciples worshiped Jesus after the calming of the storm (13:9). After Jesus had risen from the dead, He came to the disciples and they worshiped Him (Matthew 28:9, 17).

Matthew also clearly states that Jesus is the exclusive incarnation of God because He alone can be the object of faith, "All things have been handed over to Me by My Father; and no one knows the Son except the Father; nor does anyone know the Father except the Son, and anyone to whom the Son wills to reveal [Him]" (Matthew 11:27). Jesus said that the Good

News of the kingdom (the gospel of Jesus is at hand) would be preached in *all* the world as a testimony to *all* the nations (Matthew 24:14). Further, in what is known as the "Great Commission" passage of Matthew, Jesus describes the universal mission of the Church - to share the gospel message with *all* who have not yet heard it. He commands, "Go therefore and make disciples of all the nations, baptizing them in the name of the Father and the Son and the Holy Spirit, teaching them to observe all that I commanded you . . ." (Matthew 28:19-20).

LUKE AND ACTS AFFRM JESUS' DEITY

The book of Acts is an extension of Luke's first book and reveals the exclusivity of salvation through Jesus, which must be preached to the whole world, precisely as the early Christian church did, "There is salvation in no one else; for there is no other name under heaven that has been given among men by which we must be saved" (Acts 4:12). Luke describes the disciples worshiping Jesus as He ascends into Heaven: "While He was blessing them, He parted from them and was carried up into Heaven. And they, after worshiping Him, returned to Jerusalem with great joy" (Luke 24:51-52).

If Jesus is the revealed image of the living God, as these biblical passages claim, then one would expect to see evidence of similar claims for Jesus' divinity in the words and actions of the early Christians. Many of these early believers saw Jesus' miracles first hand and some even witnessed His post-resurrection appearances. As one examines even a few examples of the obviously Christocentric beliefs of the early Christian martyrs, the authenticity of the deity passages identified earlier are clearly affirmed.

AFFRMATIONS FROM EARLY CHURCH MARTYRS

The martyrdom of the apostles and many other early Christians provides background evidence for the teaching about and belief in the deity of Jesus and His exclusivity that is consistently recorded in the gospels, particularly in John. Muncaster says that "many of the 72 men appointed by Jesus in Luke 10:1 were martyred, including such people as Erastus (Romans 16:23), Aristarchus (Acts 19:29), Trophimus (Acts 21:29), Barabbas (Acts 1:23), and Ananias (Acts 9:10)."[167] Only thirty years after the death of Jesus, forceful persecution descended upon the "Jesus worshipers." The only way for them to avoid a terrifying death by wild beasts or by being burned alive was to renounce their allegiance to and worship of Christ as their God. The Emperor Trajan tried to force the Christians to "bow down to a statue of [him] and worship him to be set free. Christians continued to choose death."[168]

Tens of thousands of martyrs were buried in the catacombs of Rome in "more than 60 underground labyrinths where individual tombs and family crypts were

---

[167] Ralph O. Muncaster, *Evidence for Jesus* (Eugene: Harvest House Publishers, 1984), 69-70.
[168] Ibid.

hewn out of narrow rock passageways."[169] Some have declared that while visiting the crypts of the Christian martyrs they experienced a powerful sense of the martyrs' commitment to Christ "at a time so close to his crucifixion, when people would have strong evidence of His resurrection. Evidence of early Christian belief in Jesus as the personification of the Truth is everywhere. Symbols are prevalent throughout the catacombs."[170] If they did not lay claim to the exclusive deity of Jesus Christ and His incarnation, which were proven by His miracles and literal resurrection, then why were they martyred?

William Lane Craig states in his book, *Reasonable Faith: Christian Truth and Apologetics,* that scholars such as Moule from Cambridge and Hengel from Thüringen University have proven that the early Christians believed Jesus was God/Truth. He says they "proved that within twenty years of the crucifixion a full-blown Christology proclaiming Jesus as God incarnate existed.... The oldest

---

[169] Ibid., 72.
[170] Ibid., 73.

Christian sermon, the oldest account of a Christian martyr, the oldest pagan report of the church, and the oldest liturgical prayer (I Corinthians 16:22) all refer to Christ as Lord and God."[171]

In the early church, it was common to say that to be a witness to the resurrection of Christ was to be a martyr. In fact, the Greek word "martyrion" means 'witness' and 'martyr'.[172] Among the first martyrs of the early church were the eleven apostles of Jesus who were all eyewitnesses to the Christ events and His resurrection. The authenticity of the deity passages of Scripture and the high Christology within Paul's letters can be trusted, because the apostles lived and died as a testimony of that Truth, as did countless others after them.

There were eleven apostles that were martyred (twelve if Paul is included), and John was exiled to the Island of Patmos. Paul was beheaded in Rome between CE 67-71;

---

[171] William Lane Craig, *Reasonable Faith: Christian Truth and Apologetics* (Wheaton: Moody Press, 1984), 243.

[172] William Byron (ed.), "Foxe's Book of Martyrs" Available from, www.sacred texts.com/chr/martyrs.fox101.htm; Internet; accessed September 4, 2006.

Peter was crucified between CE 67-71; Andrew, crucified; James son of Alpheus, crucified, CE 44; Philip, crucified, CE 54; Bartholomew, crucified, CE 54; Simon,
crucified, CE 74; Matthias, stoned and beheaded; James,
brother of Jesus, killed with a fuller's club; Thomas,
killed by the spear; Matthew, slain with a halberd[173],
CE 60; and James, Son of Zebedee, beheaded, CE 44.
All 70 disciples sent out by Jesus were martyred: these
included Thaddeus, killed by arrows; Jude, crucified, 74
CE; Timothy, beaten to death, CE 97; Mark, dragged
to death.[174] Other early Christians martyred under
Domitian in 81 CE were Erastus, chamber of Corinth;
Aristarchus, the Macedonian; Trophimus, an Ephesian
converted by St. Paul; Joseph called Barsabbas, fellow-la-
bourer with Paul; and Ananias, bishop of Damascus."[175]
As the church began to spread the message of the gospel,

---

[173] A "halberd" was a weapon that combined an axe and a spear and was mounted
   on a long pole. For more information see, Fitzhenry & Whiteside, *Standard
   College Dictionary* (Toronto: Funk & Wagnall Publishing Company Limited,
   1974), 603.
[174] William Byron (ed.), "Foxe's Book of Martyrs," available from, www.sacred
   texts.com/chr/martyrs.fox101.htm; Internet; accessed; September 4, 2006.
[175] Ibid., 102.htm.

martyrdom became quite common and thus, ancient documents from their enemies provide testimony that the early Christians worshipped Jesus as God/Truth.

Affrmations from Enemies and Early Church Fathers

Pliny the Younger (CE 55-113)

Pagans during the early church period accused the Christians of worshiping Jesus as God and of worshiping a crucified sage. Twenty-two years after the death and resurrection of Jesus, a well known lawyer named Pliny the Younger had many Christians brought before him to be judged for refusing to worship the Emperor Trajan as a god. On one occasion, he wrote to Caesar that Christians met together on an appointed day "before daybreak to recite hymns antiphonally to Christ, as to a god."[176] It was common practice for a follower of Christ to worship Jesus as God incarnate and the only Savior of humanity, thus denying the validity of the Roman gods.

POLYCARP (CE 71-155)

In CE 155, Polycarp was burned at the stake in the city of Smyrna (Izmir) in modern day Turkey where he was also Bishop, because of his undying faith in Jesus Christ as the only Savior of the world. The account of his death was circulated amongst all the churches, encouraging and inspiring the many believers who would shortly face persecution. In the stadium, at one point the proconsul asked Polycarp if he would "curse the Christ" in order to be saved. Polycarp responded with a description of how much Jesus meant to him, "Eighty and six years have I served him, and he hath done me no wrong; how then can I blaspheme my king who saved

---

[176] Henry Bettenson (ed.), *Documents of the Christian Church* (New York: Oxford University Press, 1981), 4.

me?"[177] As he was about to be burned alive on a stake, he prayed, "I praise thee, I bless thee, I glorify thee, through the eternal and heavenly high priest, Jesus Christ, the beloved Son, through whom with Him and the Holy Spirit be glory now and ever and the for the ages to come. Amen."[178] In this prayer, Polycarp affirmed the pre-existence of Christ's eternal nature and declared that He is one with the Father and the Spirit, teachings that he learned from the oral tradition, Paul's letters, and his mentor, John.

IGNATIUS (CE 107)

In CE 107, Ignatius was brought to Rome to be put to death for his allegiance to Jesus Christ. In his *Evidence for Jesus,* Ralph O. Muncaster states that Ignatius was "personally acquainted with some of the apostles and had every opportunity to verify the accuracy of the life of

---

[177] Ibid., 10.

[178] J.B. Lightfoot and J.R. Harmer, *Apostolic Times* (Grand Rapids: baker Book House, 1998), 208.

Jesus through the eyewitnesses themselves."[179] During the journey from Antioch to Rome, he wrote six letters to various churches and one to Polycarp. In this letter, Ignatius alludes to Jesus as "God" twelve times and makes even more references to His exclusivity. In one of the most important references, Ignatius acknowledges the incarnation, the virgin birth, the pre-existence of Jesus as Creator, and that He is the universal King, "There is only one Physician, of the flesh and of spirit, generate and ingenerate (created and uncreated), God in man, true life in death, Son of Mary and Son of God, first passable and then impassible, Jesus Christ our Lord."[180] The fact that he wrote these seven letters within twenty years after John's death and continued to espouse the teachings of his mentor is evidence that the high Christology of Jesus' deity in the gospels did not evolve over time. Rather, it appears that John passed down what he had seen, touched, and heard as an eyewitness to the Christ-

---

[179] Ralph O. Muncaster, *Evidence for Jesus* (Eugene: Harvest House Publishers, 1984), 89.
[180] Ibid. 89

events. Let us keep on looking at more hard evidence that the early Christians saw Jesus as the personification of the Truth from the very beginning of His resurrection from the dead.

JUSTIN MARTYR (CE 100-165)

According to Moyer, between CE 100-165, a philosopher from Rome by the name of Justin Martyr met a venerable old Christian who "shook his confidence in human wisdom and pointed him to the Hebrew prophets."[181] Justin was converted to belief in Christ as God and, until he was beheaded in Rome, dedicated himself to the mission of spreading the gospel of Jesus. Like Ignatius and Polycarp, Justin proclaimed the teaching of John that Jesus is the revelation of God through His exclusive incarnation, the logos. In Justin's first apology he writes, "Jesus Christ alone has been begotten as the

---

[181] Elgin Moyer, *Wycliffe Biographical Dictionary of the Church* (Grand Rapids: Baker House, 1988), 220.

unique Son of God, being already his word, his First-begotten, and his Power."[182] "He is Himself Son of God on high, who was manifested of the Holy Spirit, came down from heaven, and being born of a Hebrew virgin took on His flesh from a virgin."[183]

IRENAEUS (CE 150-200)

Irenaeus, who was a student of Polycarp, also taught from John's gospel that Jesus is the logos incarnate and that He is the exclusive and universal savior of humanity. In his book written against heresies, Irenaeus explains that through His Word [Jesus] all His creatures learn that there is one God, the Father, who controls all things, and gives existence to all...The Word was made the minister of the Father's grace to man, for man's benefit. For

---

[182] Henry Bettenson (ed.), *Documents of the Christian Church* (New York: Oxford University Press, 1981), 60.

[183] L.G. Carey, "Justin Martyr," *The New International Dictionary of the Christian Church* (Apology 1:21-33; Dialogue with Trypho the Jew) Revised, J. D. Douglas (ed.) (Michigan: Grand Rapids, Zondervan, 1978), 133.

man he wrought his redemptive work, displaying God to man, and man to God."[184] Towards the end of the second century, Irenaeus was appointed the Bishop of Lyons in Gaul; however, he was born and educated in Asia Minor. He records that after Peter and Paul's martyrdom, Mark, who was an interpreter of Peter, wrote down the bulk of Peter's teachings about Jesus. Then Luke also wrote down the gospel as preached by his mentor Paul. In addition, "John, the disciple of the Lord, who also leaned on his breast, himself, produced his gospel, while he was living at Ephesus in [modern day Turkey] Asia."[185]

ORIGEN (CE 185-235)

Origen's "Rule of Faith," is one of the most important early church documents prior to the time of Constantine. Origen explains that this term refers to the essentials of the Christian faith as taken from the holy apostles.

---

[184] Henry Bettenson (ed.), *Documents of the Christian Church* (New York: Oxford University Press, 1981), 75-6.
[185] Ibid., 40.

Origen's first rule of faith asserts that "God is one, who created and set in order all things, and who, when nothing existed, caused the universe to be." [186] Origen describes the pre-existent Son as coming to earth from the Father and states that all things were made through Him, "He emptied Himself and was made flesh, although He was God; and being made man, He still remained what He was, namely God."[187]

TERTULLIAN (CE 160-220)

An early church father by the name of Tertullian lived shortly after the apostolic witness of Jesus Christ. He is acknowledged as one of the greatest early church apologists because of his work entitled "The Apology." Tertullian was known for his clear description of the Trinity and his continued belief in the deity of Jesus as revealed in the Scriptures to the apostles, their disciples,

---

[186] J. Stevenson (ed.), *A New Eusebeus,* Revised by W.H.C Frend (London: SPCK, 1998), 199.
[187] Ibid. 199

and then to him. He claims that they "have been taught that He (the Son) proceeds forth from God, and in that procession He is generated; so that He is the Son of God, and is called God from unity of substance with God."[188]

Amazingly, Hick denies the strong evidence of high Christology that exists in the written testimony of these earliest believers. If actions speak louder than words, then the evidence from the early believers (their worship of Jesus and their deity theology) proves that many of them understood and believed that Jesus was God/Truth and were willing to die for this belief. However, Hick believes that high Christology was accepted by the church as late as the fifth century and then lasted into the nineteenth century.[189] Hick is convinced that the church had so fully developed its deity theology that its adherents believed Jesus "had proclaimed Himself to be God, the second person of a divine Trinity, living a

[188] Russ Bush (ed.), *Classical Readings in Christian Apologetics AD 100-1800* (Grand Rapids: Baker, 1986), 92, 3.
[189] John Hick, *The Metaphor of God Incarnate* (Louisville: John Knox Press, 1993), 29.

human life; and their discipleship accordingly includes this as a central article of faith."[190] Nash counters Hick's claim, agreeing with Green's assertion that the "high view of Christ to which Hick objects can be found in documents that many scholars consider the earliest of all New Testament writings."[191] Let's take a brief look at some of this amazing evidence of Jesus being the Truth through primary sources. These early creeds were poems and songs sung and spoken by the early church followers, many of whom could not read.

PRIMARY SOURCES: PRE-SECOND COVENANT (NT) CREEDS

Moreland claims that there are many hymns and creeds within the Pauline epistles (Romans 1:3-4; 1 Corinthians 11:23ff; Philippians 2:6-11; Colossians 1:15-18; 1 Timothy 3:16) that "most scholars date ...

---

[190] Ibid. 29

[191] Ronald Nash, *Is Jesus the Only Savior?* (Grand Rapids: Zondervan Publishing House, 1994), 83.

from 33 to 48. Some, like Hengel, date many of them in the first decade after Jesus' death."[192] These early creeds and hymns contain passages and teachings referring to the resurrection of Jesus as a historical fact, and thus clearly affirm the deity of Jesus. The existence of the early creeds suggests it is highly plausible that those present at Christian assemblies memorized these doctrines and used them in their liturgy within three to five years of Jesus' resurrection. Based on this evidence, Moreland adamantly declares "the idea of a fully divine, miracle-working Jesus who rose from the dead was present during the first decade of Christianity. Such a view was not a legend which arose several decades after the crucifixion."[193]

---

[192] J.P. Moreland, *Scaling the Secular City* (Grand Rapids: Baker Book House, 1987), 148-9.
[193] Ibid.

THE CREED OF I CORINTHIANS 15:3-8

(CE 33-55)

One of the most important of the early creeds is quoted by the apostle Paul in his first letter to the Corinthians and contains testimony from eyewitnesses to the appearances of Jesus after His resurrection. It is believed to have been memorized and then written close to the time of the actual events.

> For I delivered to you as of first impor-
> tance what I also received, that Christ died
> for our sins according to the Scriptures,
> and that He was buried, and that He
> was raised on the third day according to
> the Scriptures, and that He appeared to
> Cephas, then to the twelve. After that
> He appeared to more than five hundred
> brethren at one time, most of whom
> remain until now, but some have fallen

asleep; then He appeared to James, then
to all the apostles; and last of all, as to one
untimely born, He appeared to me also. (1
Corinthians 15:3-8).

Moreland has stated "for the past one hundred years
almost all New Testament critics have accepted the
Pauline authorship of I Corinthians."[194] Leon Morris
claims that if one compares I Corinthians 15 with Acts
18, 19, and 20, "one can find strong evidence that Paul
wrote this book in CE 55 while he was still in Ephesus."[195]
If Paul wrote his letter to the Corinthians at this time, this
passage referring to eyewitnesses must have originated at
an earlier date. Gary Habermas states that there are many
reasons to indicate an early date for I Corinthians 15.
First, Paul admits that these words are not his own and
that he "received" them from another source, most likely

[194] J.P. Moreland, *Scaling the Secular City* (Grand Rapids: Baker Book House, 1987), 148-9.

[195] Gary R. Habermas, The Historical Jesus: *Ancient Evidence for the Life of Jesus*, (Nashville: Thomas Nelson Publishers, 1984), 124-150.

orally through one of the apostles who mentored him. Secondly, most scholars agree that some of the words Paul quotes from within the creed are Jewish terms that he would not have used. Thirdly, the creed is arranged in a stylized and parallel structure; thus, it seems to be an oral hymn or creed of the early church. Fourthly, the creed could have been Semitic in its origin, since it uses the Aramaic name "Cephas" for Peter. Habermas believes that Paul may have received the creed between CE 36 and 38, three years after committing his life to Jesus and shortly after his meeting with Peter and James (Galatians 1:18-19). Because of this early date and the above evidence, most theologians believe that the creed or hymn from which Paul quotes in I Corinthians 15 may have originated even earlier than Paul's conversion. If this were the case, it would be plausible, according to Habermas, that it came into existence close to the time of the resurrection itself.[196]

---

[196] Ibid., 124-150.

Although one could claim that Paul created the creed himself in order to give credence to his high Christology, this seems unlikely, since so many eyewitnesses to Jesus' post-resurrection appearances were still alive when the letter was written. If Paul had made untrue historical claims in I Corinthians 15:3-8 (500 witnesses to Jesus' post resurrection appearance), individuals who had witnessed Jesus' life and death would have countered his claims. Firstly, why did Paul give up his devout Jewish faith and his relentless desire to rid the land of all Christians in order to become a leader within the ranks of those he sought to destroy? Paul could only do what he did if he had truly experienced something amazing, something worth changing his faith and losing his reputation for. Secondly, once Paul was a Christian and began preaching that Jesus was the Son of God, (Acts 9:20) the Jews wanted him dead (v.23). Why would Paul risk everything in the presence of his new family, the followers of Christ, by stating that Jesus was God if this fact was not historically verifiable? And was not Paul's reason for wanting to persecute the Christians the same reason for which the Jews now sought Him - his belief in the deity of Jesus?

If teachings on the deity of Jesus were later developed by Paul and then added by the "unnamed" gospel writers, why is the teaching of Jesus' deity already present in the early creeds? It is obvious that Paul was not the founder of the Christian faith nor did he add to or falsify the teachings of Jesus. Paul simply agreed with all the essential declarations of Jesus' high Christology and the gospel message already present within the oral tradition. That this is true is proven by the silence of the apostles and the eyewitnesses at large, none of whom refuted his statements.

After his examination of some of the most important pre-New Testament creeds, Moreland reports, "We have historical evidence that belief in a divine Jesus was not a late, Hellenistic view of a simple Jewish prophet from Galilee. Belief in a divine Jesus was early and originated in a Jewish context."[197] Craig has commented on the Roman historian A.N. Sherwin-White who states, "Even two generations is too short a time span to allow legendary tendencies to wipe out the hard core of historical facts."[198]

These early creeds contain many reports that Jesus came from the line of David and that He lived in Nazareth, had twelve disciples, and performed many miracles. The early creeds also describe the Last Supper, Jesus' discussion with Pilate, His crucifixion in Jerusalem, and His rising from the grave in three days, appearing to many individuals and groups. The early creeds ascribe deity to Jesus and are dated well before the actual gospel writings and letters, inferring that those who followed Him did so because He had proved to them who He claimed to be. This primary evidence makes it extremely

---

[197] J. P. Moreland, *Scaling the Secular City* (Grand Rapids: Baker Book House, 1987), 150.
[198] William Lane Craig, *Reasonable Faith* (Wheaton: Cross Way Books, 1994), 285.

unlikely that a high Christology was developed over time or that Jesus did not know He was God.[199]

According to Gary Habermas, many of the creeds transmitted in the oral tradition reveal that the early Christians believed Jesus was more than a man as early as CE 30-50. Therefore, he claims, "In a real sense, the creeds preserve pre-New Testament material, and are our earliest sources for the life of Jesus."[200] Therefore, these creeds have great value because they reveal pertinent information about the life of Jesus, information that was accepted as true very close to the actual historical events. The creeds are primary testimonies passed on through oral tradition revealing what eyewitnesses saw and experienced regarding Jesus. Geisler asserts that, "perhaps even more [crucially], they reflect the preaching

---

[199]N.L. Geisler & P.K. Hoffman, *Why I Am a Christian: Leading Thinkers Explain Why they Believe* (Grand Rapids: Baker Books, 2001), 159. Some of the creedal material that summarizes these beliefs are: Luke 24:34; Acts 2:22–24, 30–32; 3:13–15; 4:10–12; 5:29–32; 10:39–41; 13:37–39; Rom. 1:3–4; 4:25; 10:9; 1 Cor. 11:23ff.; 15:3–8; Phil. 2:6–11; 1 Tim. 2:6; 3:16; 6:13; 2 Tim. 2:8; 1 Peter 3:18; 1 John 4:2.

[200] Gary R. Habermas, *The Historical Jesus: Ancient Evidence For the Life of Christ* (Joplin: College Press Publishing Company, 1996), 149.

and teaching of those who were closest to Jesus, from the earliest period of the church."[201] As one closely examines the Christological content of the creeds, it is clear that they contain the teaching of Jesus' deity and incarnation.

THE CREED OF 1 TIMOTHY 3:16

A prime example is found in the confessional creed of 1 Timothy 3:16, which is sometimes referred to as the "Christ-hymn." It indicates that the early Christians were very familiar with this material, "By common confession, great is the mystery of godliness: He who was revealed in the flesh, was vindicated in the Spirit, seen by angels, proclaimed among the nations, believed on in the world, taken up in glory" (I Timothy 3:16). Many scholars, including Moule, believe, that this particular creed because of its rhyming pattern, was used very early

---

[201] N.L. Geisler & P.K. Hoffman, *Why I Am a Christian: Leading Thinkers Explain Why they Believe* (Grand Rapids: Baker Books, 2001), 159.

in regular worship and song.[202] Thus, this creed provides evidence that followers of Jesus believed in His incarnation either already before His death or at least shortly after His resurrection. According to Habermas, Moule states that "[this creed] also presents a contrast between Jesus' human birth 'in the flesh' and his deity, further mentioning his approval by the Spirit and the witness of the angels."[203]

I have provided solid background evidence that the early Christians worshiped Jesus as God and as the only Savior of the world before and immediately after the resurrection of Jesus. Their testimony has revealed that the early Christians' understanding of Jesus corresponds with the high Christology presented in the gospels, primarily in the book of John and in Paul's letters. This concrete evidence suggests that Hick's claims are not only outdated, but that they are recklessly propagated without

---

[202] C. F. D. Moule, *The Birth of the New Testament* (Revised edition, New York: Harper and Row, 1982), 33-5.

[203] John Hick, *The Rainbow of Faiths: A Christian Theology of Religions* (Louisville: John Knox Press, 1995), 90.

careful study and adherence to historical evidence and simple laws of logic and reason. Thus, it is imperative that a response to counter Hick's two primary objections against the deity (Truth) of Jesus Christ be presented in order to affirm that traditional Christianity still has warrant to believe this primary doctrine of the early Church.

CHAPTER SIX

CONTEMPORARY RESPONSE TO JOHN HICK'S OBJECTIONS

"Jesus was well aware that He was more than a Rabbi or even a First Covenant (OT) prophet. He spoke with the authority of God, not merely the authority of a godly human being. Since He spoke with such great authority that those around him recognized His divinity, we can safely assume that He too was well aware of who He was."

- Author

RESPONSE#1: SELF-CONSCIOUSNESS OF JESUS AS TRUTH

Hick claims, "Jesus did not teach that he was God or God the Son, the second person of the Holy Trinity, incarnate. Indeed, he would probably have regarded such an idea as blasphemous!"[204] Hick believes that his rejection of Jesus' awareness of His deity is congruent with the views of most "Catholic as well as Protestant, conservative as well as liberal" theologians and that this view is the "consensus in New Testament studies today."[205] William Craig, however, counters

---

[204] John Hick, *The Rainbow of Faiths: A Christian Theology of Religions* (Louisville: John Knox Press, 1995), 90.
[205]
Ibid., 91.

Hick's assertion, claiming, "New Testament scholarship has reached something of a consensus that the historical Jesus came on the scene with an unparalleled sense of divine authority, the authority to stand and speak in the place of God Himself and to call men to repentance and faith."[206] In other words, Jesus did not have to overtly state that He was God incarnate, because He clearly proved that He had authority over all creation, whether He was in heaven or on earth. It also seems clear that His divinity was recognized and acknowledged by others because of the response of His enemies, the disciples, His apostles, and the crowds coming to hear Him. Craig and many other scholars uphold the plausibility that the testimony of Jesus recorded in 1 Timothy 2 is congruent with Jesus' view of Himself. "For there is one God, [and] one mediator also between God and men, [the] man Christ Jesus, who gave Himself as a ransom for all, the testimony [given] at the proper time (1 Timothy

---

[206] William Lane Craig, "No Other Name: A Middle Knowledge Perspective on the Exclusivity of Salvation Through Christ." *Faith and Philosophy* 6 (1989): 92.

2:5-6). What should we make of Hick's objection that Jesus never claimed His own divinity? Is it true or was He implicit through His words and actions? Hick contends that those holding to a literal incarnation doctrine "have thus had to retreat from a dominical authority for their belief to the highly debatable argument that Jesus' words and actions *implicitly* claim deity."[207] Hick seems to focus on only one issue whether or not Jesus ever uttered the exact words, I am God incarnate, consubstantiated with the Father. Beyond this, he seems to have a closed mind to any definitive evidence that could disprove his argument no matter how convincing. The fact that Jesus did not say those exact words but affirmed them in countless passages of Scripture (as listed in chapter 3) is not enough evidence for Hick or many other modern critics. They demand to know why, if Jesus was God Incarnate, He would not want to be more direct in announcing that He was God's revelation to humanity come to save

---

[207] Hick, John, "A Pluralist View" in Okholm, Dennis L. Phillips Timothy R. (eds.) *Four Views: Salvation in a Pluralistic World* (Grand Rapids: Zondervan Publishing House, 1996), 54.

the world. Yet, even if for some reason He was not able to tell the world He was God, could He not have at least told those closest to Him, His apostles and disciples?

We should not find it surprising that Jesus was indirect about His divinity, especially if we consider the strong monotheism within Judaism at the time of Christ. "Had Jesus made an outright claim to deity he would have compromised his ministry and message among both the Jews and Romans, and supplied grounds for his immediate arrest and execution by both groups."[208] Timing had to be perfect for Jesus to fulfill His mission of salvation for the world. It must also be remembered that for the Jews, claiming deity was punishable by death; likewise, the Romans would have viewed anyone making such a claim as a revolutionary, challenging the Empire.[209] The Scriptures reveal that God's timing and interaction with humanity throughout history has

---

[208] James R. Edwards, *Is Jesus the Only Savior?* (Grand Rapids: William B. Eerdmans Publishing Company, 2005), 72.

[209] E. W Stegemann and W. Stegemann, *The Jesus Movement: A Social History of Its First Century,* translated by O. C. Dean Jr. (Minneapolis: Fortress Press, 1995), 166.

been accomplished with sensitivity to the gift of free-will and the right to self-determination. God's sensitivity is consistently observed in the history of both the First Covenant (Old Testament) and the Second Covenant (New Testament). God has given freedom of choice to His creation, and His general and special revelation has always respected that boundary.

A good example of Jesus' allowing those around Him to discover for themselves who He was is found in the book of Matthew. John the Baptist was in prison, awaiting his execution at the hands of King Herod and wanted assurance that Jesus was the long awaited Messiah. Because John was about to die for preaching that the kingdom of God was at hand through Jesus, he wanted to be sure that he was dying for the Truth/Jesus. In response, Jesus sent John's disciples to John with words affirming that He was in fact the long awaited Messiah God come to humanity. But once again, God revealed Himself indirectly, allowing for human agency, just as he still grants humanity the freedom to choose the gift of salvation through faith. "Jesus answered and said to them, "Go and report to John what you hear and see: [The] blind receive sight and [the] lame walk, [the] lepers are cleansed and [the] deaf hear, the dead are raised up, and [the] poor have the gospel preached to them" (Matthew 11:4).

Here Jesus is challenging John to come to his own conclusion, just as He consistently challenged his disciples. Jesus continues to allow humanity the freedom to choose or reject Him, because without faith His saving grace has no effect. Again, it is obvious that Jesus could have used this opportunity to state that He was God incarnate, but He did not choose to do so in a direct manner. In essence, Jesus was asking His cousin and close friend John, now that you have seen and heard all this about me, what is your conclusion? Who would you say that I am by the evidence I have shown you? The verses that follow contain no response from John; thus, one concludes that he came to his own affirming conclusion and died having discovered the two most important treasures in life, knowledge of the truth, and saving faith.

THE DIVINE AUTHORITY OF JESUS/TRUTH

Jesus provided ample evidence of His divinity through His use of divine authority, thereby proving that He was self-conscious of His own divinity. This awareness was also a significant clue to others that He was God incarnate. The historical records reveal that the early church fully embraced this understanding of His divinity. For example, John 10:36 and 19:7 record that His claims to divinity were so evident that the Jewish leaders accused Him of blasphemy, threatening to kill Him. At His crucifixion, Jesus also claimed to be the Son of God as His enemies mocked Him using His own words, "He trusts in God; let God rescue [Him] now, if He delights in Him; for He said, 'I am the Son of God'" (Matthew 27:43).

Jesus was well aware that He was more than a Rabbi or even an Old Testament prophet. He spoke with the authority of God, not merely the authority of a godly human being. Since He spoke with such great authority that those around Him recognized his divinity, we can safely assume that He too was well aware of who He was. It is true that other teachers and prophets saw themselves as representing all the Jewish people when they spoke and that some even spoke on behalf of God; however, they never spoke with the authority of God. The prophets would declare, "Thus says the Lord," but no writer describes the prophets in the same way as Mark 1:22 describes the reaction of the crowd to Jesus, "They were amazed at His teaching; for He was teaching them as [one] having authority, and not as the scribes."

JESUS' AUTHORITY OVER THE SABBATH

Jesus continued to reveal who He was to those who were interested by claiming to have authority over the

Sabbath. Mark 2:27-28 records that, "Jesus said to them, 'The Sabbath was made for man, and not man for the Sabbath. So the Son of Man is Lord even of the Sabbath.'" When Jesus declared His authority over the Sabbath and "even violated its ordinates by plucking grain (Mark 3:23-26) and healing on the Sabbath (Mark 1:21-28; 3:1-6; John 9:14) he personally enacted the authority of the Creator who instituted the Sabbath."[210] By these actions and words, Jesus provided major clues that He was the unique revelation of God incarnated in the flesh.

JESUS' AUTHORITY OVER THE SPIRIT WORLD

Jesus continued to prove to those around Him that He was God by demonstrating His complete authority not only over the physical world but also over the spiritual world. Significantly, the evil spirits (demons or fallen angels) knew exactly who Jesus was and described

---

[210] James R. Edwards, *Is Jesus the Only Savior?* (Grand Rapids: William B. Eerdmans Publishing Company, 2005), 77.

Him as the "Son of God" in nearly every encounter they had with Him (Mark 1:24; 3:11; Luke 4:41). At the end of each encounter, Jesus was victorious and spoke with the authority of God when He exorcised or reprimanded them. Even the demons themselves begged Him for mercy "Mark 5:7", as they would their Master and Creator. "With a shriek, he screamed, "Why are you interfering with me, Jesus, Son of the Most High God? In the name of God, I beg you, don't torture me!""

JESUS' AUTHORITY OVER NATURE AND DISEASE

The miracles of Jesus are clues of His divinity and are described throughout the Second Covenant (NT). To deny the reality of these supernatural, miraculous events in Jesus' life is to deny that God has directly revealed Himself in human history. Miracles play a major role in the two Covenants because they reveal God's total control over all His creation; this message is also communicated through the actions of Jesus. In the Second Covenant, the records of the miracles of Jesus are predominant because God wants all humanity to know the life-changing power that comes only through Jesus Christ. Yet Hick rejects any of the miracles described in the New Testament, even though they are major evidence that Jesus was in fact God - the physical presence of Truth. Hick concurs with the theologians of the Jesus Seminar whose "conclusions are based on radical presuppositions, one of which is an unjustified rejection of any miraculous intervention in history by God."[211] To deny the existence of Jesus' miracles is also to deny why He had so many followers in the first place.

The miracles of Jesus, cumulating with His resurrection, were the major reasons the early Christians and the historical church continued to follow Him, even unto death. Jesus healed human bodies of tangible and visible diseases such as leprosy that cannot be reasoned away

---

[211] Norman L. Geisler, *Baker Encyclopedia of Christian Apologetics* (Grand Rapids: Baker, 1998), 388.

by psychological explanations or by placing ones head in the sand and pretending such do not exist. (Matthew 8:2-4; Mark 1:40-45; Luke 5:12-16). Jesus also demonstrated that He had the authority to revoke the power of death, a power that only God the Creator could have had (Matthew 9:18-26; Mark 5:21; John 6:40, 44, 54). Jesus also had complete power and control over nature, evidence that Jesus was God, since only the Creator could speak to what He had made and command it to do what He said (Matthew 8:23-27; Mark 4:35). Jesus walked where only God could walk on water (Matthew 14:25), and He made food appear out of thin air (Mark 6:30).

JESUS' AUTHORITY TO FORGIVE SINS

If Jesus was not aware of His own deity, why would He have used God's authority to forgive sins? Hick suggests that Jesus never used God's authority to forgive the sins of humanity, asking, did Jesus actually "abrogate the Torah, and did he in fact do what God can do in forgiving

sinners?"[212] He then continues his argument by quoting
Sanders, who believes that Jesus "only pronounced forgiveness, which is not the prerogative of God, but of the
priesthood."[213] Hick should be well aware that first, the
Protestant church rejects the belief that a priest or any
other human being can forgive the sins of another on
their own. Secondly, the priests of the First Covenant
(OT) gave a sacrifice on behalf of the people; however,
they never had the authority to forgive what only God
could forgive through the sacrifice. The Scriptures state
that mere human beings do not have authority to forgive sins on their own merit because "all have sinned and
fall short" of God's glory - perfection (Roman 3:23; 1
John 1:9). The only way Jesus could forgive the sins of
another human being would be if He were the holy and
sinless God/Truth become man incarnate. The Second
Covenant (NT) is clear that believers may indirectly for-

---

[212] John Hick, *The Metaphor of God Incarnate* (Louisville: John Knox Press, 1993), 28.
[213] Ronald Nash, *Is Jesus the Only Savior?* (Grand Rapids: Zondervan Publishing House, 1994), 83.

give the sins of others, but only in the name of the One who was able to atone for the sins of humanity by His own sinlessness Jesus/Truth. Hick needs to pay attention to the reaction of the Jewish leaders who believed that only God had the authority to forgive sins, these leaders clearly condemned Jesus for forgiving sins using His own authority. Why would the Scribes and Pharisees accuse Jesus of blasphemy if He did not do what, in their eyes, only God could possibly do? Luke 5:21 reports, "The scribes and the Pharisees began to reason, saying, 'Who is this [man] who speaks blasphemies? Who can forgive sins, but God alone?'" Matthew 9:6 states, "'but so that you may know that the Son of Man has authority on earth to forgive sins' then He said to the paralytic, 'Get up, pick up your bed and go home.'" The Jewish leaders were angry with Jesus not only because He forgave the sins of the paralytic but also because Jesus forgave him by His own authority, thus claiming equality with God. Through this demonstration of His authority, Jesus was claiming for Himself the sinlessness of God and suggesting that He was in fact God incarnate. In every passage where Jesus revealed His authority to forgive the sins of others, He "acted as though the sins against other humans were violations of His holy law and thus against Him as well."[214]

Now, you may be wondering how it would be possible to know that Jesus was without sin, since any person can make such a claim. While this may be a valid question, it would be something quite different for someone to actually prove this claim, especially since close friends and relatives would be likely to refute it. However, individuals who knew Jesus very intimately for a number of years did testify to His sinlessness. Peter describes Jesus metaphorically as a spotless lamb (1 Peter 1:19) and verifies that He never spoke a sinful word (2:22). Paul "adds to his testimony the unanimously expressed belief of the first Christians that Jesus was sinless" (1 Corinthians

---

[214] Ronald Nash, *Is Jesus the Only Savior?* (Grand Rapids: Zondervan Publishing House, 1994), 83.

5:21).[215] In John's gospel, Jesus Himself claims He was without sin, challenging His accusers by asking which of them could convict Him of sin; in response, they remain silent (John 8:46). No one, not even His enemies, could successfully prove that Jesus committed a single sin; thus it is reasonable to conclude that Jesus was who He claimed to be - God incarnate, the personification of Truth. As Geisler declares, "What man can live a consistently sinless life when viewed at such close range?"[216]

AUTHORITY OVER HIS OWN DEATH: THE RESURRECTION

Hick contends that the Jesus deity movement developed shortly after Jesus' death, around the time of the "event we call the resurrection [that] adopted both these ideas [doctrine of salvation and resurrection] and

[215] Norman L. Geisler, Baker *Encyclopedia of Christian Apologetics* (Grand Rapids: Baker, 1998), 345.
[216] Ibid., 348.

eventually fused them together."[217] However, the evidence presented in chapter five has demonstrated that the historical facts do not support Hick's conclusions. It is obvious that prior to His death and resurrection Jesus taught that He was God incarnate come to earth for the salvation of the world and even predicted the final events. While He did not say He was God in the exact words Hick demands, His words of authority and His miraculous actions changed the lives of thousands of men and women around the world. Jesus touched their lives in such an extensive way that they were willing to testify that He was God before a hostile world. Encountering Jesus transformed monotheistic Jewish leaders into followers of Jesus unto the death.

Thus, one can argue that Jesus' life-changing impact was the loudest self-claiming proclamation Jesus could have ever made that He was God incarnate. Jesus declared that He was God come to earth through His resurrection

---

[217] John Hick, *A Rainbow of Faiths: A Christian Theology of Religion*, (Louisville: John Knox, 1995), 91.

from the dead. His resurrection was His voice shouting from the rooftops that He was the flesh of God fulfilling His mission to be the atonement for the entire world and that to deny it would be to deny Him. Sir Norman Anderson says of the resurrection, "Both the deity of Jesus and the efficacy of His atoning death were, more-over, proved for the apostles by the fact of His resurrection."[218] He asserts that the disciples were so impacted by their experiences with Jesus and His teachings that their first response after the resurrection was to tell others the gospel message and to encourage everyone to worship Him. They knew instinctively the unity between Jesus and Yahweh by applying "to Jesus Old Testament verses which, in origin, clearly applied to Yahweh alone, and felt free without any qualm of idolatry to worship Jesus and to address him directly in prayer."[219] What else but this recognition of Jesus' divinity could possibly account

[218]
Sir Norman Anderson, *Christianity and World Religions: The Challenge of Pluralism* (Downers Grove: Inter-Varsity Press, 1984), 47.
[219] Ibid., 113.

for the overwhelming joy the early church experienced and the unprecedented growth in numbers that occurred immediately after the resurrection of Jesus Christ? Hick claims that after the death of Jesus the apostles and five hundred disciples experienced visions or hallucinations in which Jesus appeared to them. Yet, he admits that something out of the ordinary had transformed the followers of Jesus:

> In the days after Jesus' crucifixion, something momentous happened to bring the disciples' faith back to life, and indeed to more than its former life; and according to the account of the Christian community itself that momentous event was the resurrection of Jesus to life that was mysteriously more than his former life. He was present now in such a way that they no longer doubted his lordship. And so

his resurrection became the foundation of their faith.[220]

While Hick acknowledges that something extraordinary occurred after the "apparent" resurrection, he does not believe that Jesus literally rose from the dead, contrary to the many Scriptures that speak of eyewitnesses. Instead, he claims that if one's friend had risen from the dead, one would not suddenly believe that this "acquaintance was divine, or that a stamp of authenticity had been placed on all he ever said or did...."[221] In other words, he declares that this "apparent" event does not prove Jesus was God.

In Hick's eyes, many other things must be affirmed before one can conclude that Jesus was divine. What then would those "other" affirmations be? If a friend claims to have died but is now obviously alive and well, the first thing one must verify is whether he or she had

[220] John Hick, *God Has Many Names* (Philadelphia: Westminster Press, 1982), 24.
[221] Ibid., 64.

actually died in the first place. If one could discover that in fact this friend had died, the next logical response would be to make sure the friend was truly alive. If this could also be verified, then it would be wise to take a close look at the character of this friend to ascertain whether a label of divinity could plausibly be applied. However, we know that no human being in the history of the world other than the Jesus of history and faith presented in the gospel accounts could pass these tests and be raised to life after three days in the tomb. Thus, we must conclude, contrary to Hick, that since Jesus meets all these requirements, He is Truth.

The disciples clearly believed Jesus was God; they came to this conclusion not because they needed Him to be God or because His deity was a developed doctrine, but because His life had so affected them that His divinity was an obvious conclusion. Anderson says that the early Christians believed in Jesus' divinity immediately "because of their experience with Him; there was something about His earthly life which made the resurrection, once it had happened, seem the natural, proper and convincing sequel."[222]

It seems Hick assumes that everyone will agree his Christology is fundamentally based on historical (i.e., that Jesus did not himself teach His incarnation) and theological (i.e., that his two natures cannot be explained) appraisals. However, according to Pinnock, "It seems more likely that this analysis is a rationalization of the position his system requires. Readers have been told that Hick made his move to pluralism before the problem of Jesus was solved."[223] I wonder if any amount of evidence or clues pointing to Jesus' self-claimed divinity would have satisfied Hick's dogmatic stance. In Pinnock's opinion, Hick's need to negate the incarnation has more to do with his ideology than with evidence, no matter how convincing. "Be clear for Hick, Jesus cannot

---

[222] Sir Norman Anderson, *Christianity and World Religions: The Challenge of Pluralism* (Downers Grove: Inter-Varsity Press, 1984), 76.

[223] Pinnock, Clark H., "A Pluralist View: Response to John Hick," in Dennis L. Okholm & Timothy R. Phillips, (eds.), *More Than One Way: Four Views on Salvation in a Pluralistic World* (Grand Rapids: Harper Collins Publishers, 1995), 63.

be more than an inspiring example, whatever the evidence is! The bias against the Incarnation is invincible going in."[224]

Hick believed the disciples did extraordinary things after Jesus' death; however, Carruthers points out that Hick denies "the central significance Jesus' resurrection has for faith. The only Jesus ever known and experienced was the earthly Jesus. Christian faith is the same faith that the disciples had before the death of Jesus."[225] Carruthers also asserts that, significantly, in reducing the biblical life of Jesus to His earthly life, "Hick can only account for the 'newness' of Christian faith after the resurrection as the beginning of a deification process, a process that results merely from human needs."[226] However, it has been clearly shown that even in the primitive Christology existing prior to Paul's letters, the resurrec-

---

[224] Ibid.

[225] Gregory H. Carruthers, S. J., *The Uniqueness of Jesus Christ in the Theocentric Model of the Christian Theology of World Religions: An Elaboration and Evaluation of the Position of John Hick* (Lanham: University Press of America, Inc. 1990), 160.

[226] Ibid.

tion event was the core of the Christian declaration that Jesus was God incarnate.

Thus, Hick's declaration that Jesus did not claim His own divinity is unwarranted. However, one more issue needs to be addressed before warranted belief in Jesus as Truth can be declared.

RESPONSE #2: PORTRAIT OF JESUS: INSEPARABLE IN HISTORY AND FAITH

Hick's second argument denies the authenticity of any self-claim passages attributed to Jesus or high Christocentric theology found in the New Testament. His core argument can be summarized thus: "The New Testament documents were written during the early stages of this development and contain both flashbacks to the human Jesus of history and anticipations of the divine Christ of later official church doctrine."[227]

---

[227] Hick, John, "A Pluralist View" in Okholm, Dennis L. Phillips Timothy R. (eds.) *Four Views: Salvation in a Pluralistic World* (Grand Rapids: Zondervan Publishing House, 1996), 35.

He would also say that "The four gospels must not be looked at as eyewitnesses to a historical event like out of a newspaper, but written by people that were not present."[228]

Carruthers asserts, that since Hick "reduces the Christ-event to the earthly life of Jesus, he is not in fact dealing with the full Christ-event which formed the foundation of subsequent faith and theology."[229] Hick's contention is that the Christological evolution of the Second Covenant (New Testament) was the result of humanity's need for a Savior and does not in the end stand up to common sense. From the beginning, the goal of Christological maturation was to express God's self communication in the quite unsurpassable and final way that was Jesus. This Christological development already had begun during the earthly life of Jesus, but since the full revelation of Jesus was not complete during

---

[228] Ibid.

[229] Gregory H. Carruthers, S. J., *The Uniqueness of Jesus Christ in the Theocentric Model of the Christian Theology of World Religions: An Elaboration and Evaluation of the Position of John Hick* (Lanham: University Press of America, Inc. 1990), 203.

His earthly life, neither was the Christian faith complete. Therefore, neither could Christology be complete. Only with the resurrection of Jesus and the sending of the Spirit, would the Christ-event and Christian faith reach its fullness.[230]

The early church had affirmed the deity of Jesus and demonstrated this belief, through words and actions, by CE 30, (or earlier if one includes oral transmission of the creeds). Many scholars agree that Paul's letters contain a high Christology, yet they are some of the earliest Biblical manuscripts found in the Second Covenant (NT). Why then does Hick still believe that the deity of Christ was a metaphysical theory that evolved only at the end of the first century?

In the writings of R. Bultmann and the conclusions of the Jesus Seminar, Hick has found justification for doubting the authenticity of John's gospel. He totally denies that any high Christology is authentic within the Scriptures, claiming it is a developed faith theology.

---

[230]Ibid., 205.

Hick appropriates Bultmann's critical form method to separate the doctrinal layers of faith from what actually occurred in history. The New Testament records, argues Hick, "are all documents of faith," and thus must be separated or removed from what is historical.[231] By confusing faith and theology, Hick "has impoverished the nature and the role of faith itself."[232] Evidence exists within the gospels that doctrines such as the incarnation, although they may have been primitively articulated, were not developed over time by ghostwriters. After an intense study of the Second Covenant (New Testament) data, Howard Marshall concludes, "The view that it [the incarnation] is found merely on the fringe of the New Testament is a complete travesty of the facts."[233] It is

---

[231] Hick, John, "A Pluralist View" in Okholm, Dennis L. Phillips Timothy R. (eds.) *Four Views: Salvation in a Pluralistic World* (Grand Rapids: Zondervan Publishing House, 1996), 35.

[232] Gregory H. Carruthers, S. J., *The Uniqueness of Jesus Christ in the Theocentric Model of the Christian Theology of World Religions: An Elaboration and Evaluation of the Position of John Hick* (Lanham: University Press of America, Inc. 1990), 251.

[233] Marshall, Howard I., "Incarnational Christology in the New Testament," In H. H. Rowdon (ed.), *Christ the Lord,* (Leicester: Inter-Varsity Press, 1982), 13.

obvious that the Christological doctrine of the incarnation is clearly the foundational teaching within John's gospel, Paul's letters, Hebrews, and 1 Peter.[234] Dunn believes that radical form critics have subjected Jesus to a fine detail-critique and "reconstruction without adequate appreciation of the extent to which that damaged the whole picture."[235] He goes on to say that projects such as the Jesus seminar do not have the full picture of Jesus because they have completely left out the aspect of faith.

Hick believes the most crucial question to ask about the passages that seem to refer to Jesus' deity is "whether they are from Jesus Himself or if they have been touched up [redacted] to express the belief of the Gospel writers; and this is something impossible definitively to determine."[236] If Hick truly believes that one cannot "definitively determine" whether or not the gospel writers

---

[234] Ibid., 176.

[235] James Dunn, *A New Perspective on Jesus: What the Quest for the Historical Jesus Missed* (Grand Rapids: Baker Academic, 2005), 12.

[236] John Hick, *A Rainbow of Faiths: A Christian Theology of Religions* (Louisville: John Knox, 1995), 97 (Italics Mine).

added the theology of Jesus' deity, how can he then be so definitive in his belief that a major redaction occurred and thus conclude that Jesus never claimed His own deity. According to Hick, Matthew, Mark, and Luke are called the synoptic gospels because they are so closely aligned with each other; however, John's gospel is very different in its character. In contrast to the synoptic sayings of Jesus and His parables, John "often speaks in long theological discourses, and the theology embodied in them is much more developed in the direction of what became Christian orthodoxy than in the synoptics."[237] However, for Hick to make such a serious accusation that crucially challenges Christocentric theology is irresponsible and even reckless.

---

[237] John Hick, *What Does the Bible Really Say?* A sermon preached at Carrs Lane URC church, Birmingham, July 2005, available from http://www.johnhick.org.uk/, Internet; accessed; November 18th, 2005.

AUTHENTICITY OF HIGH CHRISTOLOGY WITHIN THE SCRIPTURES

HIGH CHRISTOLOGY AND JOHN'S GOSPEL

The complete evidence for the historical reliability of John's gospel cannot be covered in this chapter, because a study of such magnitude would require a number of different books.[238] However, this chapter will provide evidence challenging the validity of Hick's theory of an early gradualistic Christology.

---

[238] Providing a thorough study of evidence for the historical reliability of John's gospel is not the intent or purpose of this thesis. To do so would be to repeat the work of all the scholars who have so adequately defended its authenticity; however, readers should examine recent works by Craig Blomberg, *The Historical Reliability of John's Gospel* (Downers Grove: Inter-Varsity Press, 2001); *The Historical Reliability of the Gospels* (Downers Grove: Inter-Varsity Press, 1987). Chapter four of this book contains a list of notable scholars who have recently argued in favor of the reliability of the gospels.

M. Hunter asserts that there are many reasons for believing the existing Christ-event in all the gospels, including John's, is reliable:

1) The earliest believers were Jews who were very careful about faithfully preserving the initial traditions of Jesus' life and teachings;

2) The Gospel authors were 'in a position to know the facts about Jesus';

3) Jesus taught in such a manner that his teachings could be more easily remembered;

4) All four Gospels correctly reflect the first-century Palestinian milieu;

5) In spite of differences, the same portrait of Jesus emerges from each of the four Gospels.[239]

Contrary to Hick's claims, many modern scholars, both Catholic and Protestant, have convincingly defended the reliability of the gospel of John, believing

---

[239] A. M. Hunter, *Jesus Lord and Savior* (Grand Rapids: Eerdmans, 1976), 39-40.

that John, the original apostle and an eyewitness to the Jesus-events, is clearly its author. Blomberg, a well-respected scholar, argues that "every piece of ancient, external evidence, save one, agrees that the author was the apostle John, the son of Zebedee."[240] He states that recently, complete commentaries and articles defending much of the historicity of John's gospel have appeared; however, they have been ignored and remain virtually unchallenged by liberals.[241]

It is evident that John's disciples used his book in their writings, since they clearly incorporate metaphors such as Jesus the "Logos" or Jesus the "light" that shines in the "darkness." John's disciple Polycarp alludes to 1 John 4:2 and uses similar language to that found in John's gospel. Justin Martyr refers to John 3:3-5 and "speaks of the gospels as including 'memoirs of the apostles' in the plural," which can only mean that he was talking about Matthew

---

[240]Craig Blomberg, *The Historical Reliability of John's Gospel: Issues and Commentary* (Downers Grove: Inter-Varsity Press, 2001), 25.
[241] Ibid.

and John (Mark and Luke were not apostles).²⁴² In addition, Irenaeus gives a clear description of all four gospels and alludes to John as "the disciple of our Lord."²⁴³
Therefore, "the variety of contexts in which Irenaeus
refers to John and /or his gospels demonstrates that it
was already commonly believed around the empire that
the son of Zebedee authored this work."²⁴⁴

HIGH CHRISTOLOGY IN PAUL'S LETTERS

Admittedly, within a few short years after the resurrection and the emergence of the early church, various
heresies and false doctrines were already in existence.
In Paul's day, many false witnesses, i.e. the Gnostics,
preached a distorted doctrine and a warped Christology
(1 Timothy 4:20, 21; 6:3; 2 Corinthians 11:13; Galatians
2:4; 2 Peter 2:1). However, Hick denies that Paul is
the original author of most letters ascribed to him and

---

²⁴² Ibid., 24.
²⁴³ Ibid
²⁴⁴ Ibid

claims that redaction occurred in them. He bases these claims on weak or miniscule evidence, saying that Paul could not have been their author, since his "language moves in the direction of deification."[245] As one reads Paul's letters, it is obvious that Paul's Christology more than moves in that direction; in nearly every paragraph, he blatantly affirms that Jesus is God and that the apostles agree with his theology.

One of the world's leading New Testament scholars, Martin Hengel, does not believe Hick's evidence adequately supports his graduated Christological theory. Hengel states, "The time between the death of Jesus and the fully developed Christology that we find in the earliest Christian documents, the letters of Paul, is so short that the development which takes place within it can be called amazing."[246] J. P. Moreland agrees with Hengel's view that there does not appear to be any evolutionary expansion of Jesus' deity within the letters of

---

[245] John Hick, *The Metaphor of God Incarnate: Christology in a Pluralistic Age* (Louisville: John Knox Press, 1993), 43

[246] Martin Hengel, *Between Jesus and Paul* (Philadelphia: Fortress, 1983), 31.

Paul. Moreland states that from Paul's letters one can presume "that the picture of a fully divine, miracle working Jesus was not one that developed several decades after his death. Indeed, a full-blown Christology was present no later than fifteen years after the crucifixion."[247] If Hick is correct in saying that the early church developed the deity doctrine, then it could be said that the early Christians who worshipped Jesus as God were committing idolatry. Carruthers asserts that, "With the strong Jewish roots of the early disciples, it's hard to accept they could engage in such a process without being aware that that was what they were doing, and without some of their number objecting."[248]

---

[247] J. P. Moreland, *Scaling the Secular City: A Defense of Christianity* (Grand Rapids: Baker Book House, 1987), 148.

[248] Gregory H. Carruthers, S. J., *The Uniqueness of Jesus Christ in the Theocentric Model of the Christian Theology of World Religions: An Elaboration and Evaluation of the Position of John Hick* (Lanham: University Press of America, Inc.1990), 251.

FROM IMPLICIT TO EXPLICIT

CHRISTOLOGY

SON OF GOD OR GOD THE SON?

Hick assumes that the writers of John's gospel came to a wrong conclusion about the phrase "Son of God," thus developing the notion of Jesus' eternal and pre-existent divinity. Hick believes that the Biblical use of the language of divine sonship does not allow one to conclude that Jesus was divine. According to Hick, the Council of Nicaea shifted the meaning of the term "Son of God" from being metaphorical to being metaphysical: "The poetic title 'Son of God' becomes the philosophical 'God the Son.' Nicaea, according to Hick, misunderstood this mythological meaning and treated it as a literal or metaphysical meaning."[249] Hick's assumption is totally unwarranted. While Hick correctly determines that the title "Son of God" in and of itself does not

---

[249] Ibid., 223.

warrant a conclusion to Jesus' divinity, he cannot prove that it does not refer to Jesus' deity. Where is Hick's evidence that Nicaea misunderstood anything?

The Scriptures are just as clear about Jesus' deity as later church theology: they are just not as mature in their Christological understanding. In time, doctrines articulating a high Christology did become more developed, but the deity doctrines are not as obscure in the gospels as Hick claims. Bernard Lonergan explains, "What Mark, Paul, and John thought about Christ was neither confused nor obscure, but quite clear and distinct; yet their teaching acquired a new kind of clarity through the definition of Nicaea."[250] In other words, it is logical that the church's understanding of Jesus' divinity and related doctrines would mature; however, this maturation was based on the cornerstone of historical Truth already existing within the gospels.

---

[250] Bernard Lonergan, *The Way to Nicaea: The Dialectical Development of Trinitarian Theology* (London: Dalton, Longman & Todd, 1976), 13.

Hick contends that the evolution of the term the "Son of God" into "God the Son" is evidence of how the church creates doctrine. However, Dunn argues that "the understanding of Jesus as Son of God apparently did not provide the starting point for a Christology of pre-existence or incarnation."[251] I strongly believe that High Christology was obviously present from the beginning of Jesus' ministry, and, over time, the church was able to explain it in more detail and clarity. If Hick would carefully examine the intent of the passages containing the terms "Son of God" and "Son of Man," he would have to concur that accepting Jesus as being "God the Son" is not difficult. In fact, after one examines only a few "Son of God" and "Son of Man" passages, it becomes evident that the intentions of the authors were to affirm the high Christology present throughout the New Testament.

As a title, it is evident from examples in the New Testament that the use of the term "Son of God" in the

---

[251] James Dunn, *Christology in the Making: A New Testament Inquiry in the Origins of the Doctrine of the Incarnation* (London: SCM, 1980), 64.

First Covenant (Old Testament) was also rare, particularly in Jewish circles. When the Jewish leaders asked if Jesus claimed to be the "Son of God" and He answered "yes," they believed He should be put to death (Matthew 26:63). In the book of Mark, the high priest asks Jesus if He is the "Messiah, the Son of the blessed God?" Jesus replies, "I am, and you will see me, the Son of Man, sitting at God's right hand in the place of power and coming back on the clouds of heaven" (Mark 14: 60-62). After Jesus' reply, the Jewish leaders want to kill him, not for being a man who was close to God or one who had a special mission, but because they realize, He is claiming His own deity.

The gospels use the term "Son of God" or variations of it to refer to Jesus; for example, at His birth, the angel Gabriel calls Jesus: "the Son of the Most High" and the "Son of God" (Luke 1:32-35). In Matthew 4, the devil twice challenges Jesus, asking him, "Are you the "Son of God?" (Matthew 4:3,6). In Mark, even the unclean spirits recognize who Jesus is since they confer divine

Sonship upon Him (Mark 3:11). The apostle Peter affirms His deity, calling Jesus "the Christ, the Son of the Living God," obviously inferring His pre-existence, (Matthew 16:16). Thus, the biblical context in which the phrase "Son of God" is used clearly infers a high Christology and, at times, ascribes to Jesus' authority or equality with God. The phrase "Son of God" is, therefore, much more than a common term used for a person of royalty, authority, or mission, as Hick contends. It is evidence that Jesus was who He said He was, the Truth.

CHAPTER SEVEN

ADDITIONAL EVIDENCE THAT JESUS IS TRUTH

"The Jesus of history and faith is the personification of Truth without an 's.'"

- Author

EYEWITNESS TESTIMONIES

THE LIFEBLOOD OF THE ORAL TRADITION

An eyewitness account of an event is the most powerful testimony in a court of law and in an oral tradition. While Hick does not completely deny the existence of eyewitnesses to the Christ-events, he discredits the reality of what they observed. How can he claim that someone has lied about an eyewitness event when he has no primary evidence to bring as counter evidence. Hick is also aware that if any of the New Testament writers were eyewitnesses as they claim, it would greatly weaken his objections against the doctrine of Jesus' deity being a gradually developed Christocentric theology.

Hick denies that any of the scriptural writers were eye-witnesses to Jesus' resurrection. He argues, "According to the consensus, none of them [New Testament books] was in fact written by an eye witness."[252] However, he bases his assumptions solely on the outdated scholarship of radical liberal theologians, who from the onset were anti-supernaturalists denying Jesus' deity, his resurrection, and any other counter-evidence presented by respected conservative biblical scholars. He neglects the eyewitnesses who would have scrutinized every word of Jesus, making sure that what was affirmed and written was true to the community accounts of the oral Jesus tradition.

Paul, a strict monotheist, had originally persecuted the followers of Jesus shortly after the resurrection. He was miraculously converted to Jesus and was taught the

---

[252] John Hick, "What Does the Bible Really Say?" A sermon preached at Carrs Lane URC church, Birmingham, July 2005, available from http://www.johnhick.org.uk/; Internet; accessed November 18th, 2005.

Jesus tradition by the apostles. If the high Christology within Paul's letters had been contrary to the Jesus tradition or if Paul's understanding of Jesus had in any way contradicted the accounts of eyewitnesses, surely he would have been refuted by the followers of Jesus, as well as by the apostles who had to sanction Paul's teaching before he began to spread the message of Jesus (Acts 9:27,28) to the Gentiles. Therefore, it seems likely that the high Christology in Paul's letters was the same as the apostles' understanding of Jesus' deity. Paul passed on to the Gentiles what he had been taught; thus, his "Hellenistic" Christocentric theology must have originated with the Jewish apostles and did not gradually develop, as Hick claims.

Paul wrote what had been passed on to him from the apostles - that Jesus the Truth died for the sins of humanity and rose from the grave on the third day. He testified that Jesus was seen by Peter, James, then by the twelve, and finally, simultaneously, by more than five hundred of his followers, most of whom were still alive when Paul was writing (1 Corinthians 15:1-7). Thus, Paul's testimony and high Christology would have been easily verifiable by eyewitnesses and the original apostles.

THE ARGUMENT FROM CREDULITY

Hick argues the church has not proven the historical accuracy of the deity of Jesus and His resurrection, yet there is more evidence for the reliability of the gospels than for most historical events. Evans argues, "The criterion rests on the common sense principle that if more than one source testifies to a particular event, then it is more likely to be historical. However, why is this principle or test not required equally with other historical sources?"[253] If this test were required in every single case involving historical records, most of the major historical sources assumed to be reliable would be deemed suspect. However, Hick wants the burden of proof to reside

---

[253] Steven C. Edwards, *The Historical Christ and the Jesus of Faith: The Incarnation Narrative as History* (Oxford: Clarendon Press, 1996), 330.

with the gospels so he can create his hypothesis that the church's belief in the deity doctrines was developed over time. He can then create blanket statements such as that the gospel writers were not eyewitnesses to the Christ-events or that Jesus made no claims to be God incarnate.

In Evans' opinion, Hick's skepticism functions on two levels. "First, there is a general skepticism about historical testimony, and secondly, a specific skepticism about the gospel testimonies, since they come from Christian sources, and thus are biased in a number of ways."[254]

Yet Hick will not give the benefit of the doubt to evidence that eyewitnesses actually penned the witnessed event, even when they testify to this witness in the document itself. If someone testifies to having witnessed a historical event, he or she must be believed unless there is equal or greater evidence that shows otherwise. John was with Jesus from the beginning, and he testified to

[254] Ibid.

what he had seen with his own eyes, heard with his own ears, and touched with his own hands.

What was from the beginning, what we have heard, what we have seen with our eyes, what we have looked at and touched with our hands, concerning the Word of Life and the life was manifested, and we have seen and testify and proclaim to you the eternal life, which was with the Father and was manifested to us what we have seen and heard we proclaim to you also, so that you too may have fellowship with us; and indeed our fellowship is with the Father, and with His Son Jesus Christ. *These things we write*, so that our joy may be made complete. This is the message *we have heard from Him* and announce to you, that God is Light, and in Him there is no darkness at all. (1 John 1:1-5), (italics mine).

This eyewitness testimony must be believed unless Hick can provide solid counter evidence of equal or greater value, yet he has nothing to present but theories that attack and deny the authenticity of the witnesses. To challenge an eyewitness's testimony is a serious matter in any culture; therefore, Hick must present evidence from at least one eyewitness countering John's eyewitness account. This witness would have to know John and have evidence that either the events John described did not occur the way John claimed or that he did not say the words attributed to him in the first place. However, Hick has no counter witnesses, basing his entire case against John on old theories and his own biased presuppositions. Without providing any solid, credible evidence to counter the apostle John's eyewitness accounts, I believe Hick's case would be thrown out of any court of law in the free world.

If you examine 1 John 1:1-5, John uses first hand accounts an amazing number of times. It is clear that the beloved apostle is doing his best to convince his readers that he is telling them the truth. His words are true, he says, because "we" (including eyewitnesses other than himself, possibly the apostles) were witnesses to the Christ-events and are passing on to the church the very words presented by the Truth, Jesus Himself. This evidence should be more than enough to make Hick reconsider the validity of Jesus' deity and of the literal resurrection. Yet instead of applying the rational principle of credulity, Hick would sooner ignore the eyewitness testimonies, and repeat his denial of an early high Christology without counter evidence.

Hick's claims that the church manipulated the accounts of Jesus and that no documents were written by eyewitnesses to the Christ-events are not congruent with the historical evidence. Therefore, unless Hick proves a different scenario than is evidently present in the historical documents, Christians are warranted to believe that Jesus' disciples saw Him as God/Truth and that His deification was not developed later by the church. Edwards is convinced the "interpretation that the first early Christians put upon the life, ministry, and death of Jesus does not appear to have originated in their minds at all, but in the mind and heart of Jesus." [255] This evidence suggests that it would be implausible to believe that all of the scriptural references to Jesus' divinity were slowly redacted by later writers and not penned by the original authors. If the deity doctrine was developed over time, "How, then, did the early church, dispersed in space and time throughout the ancient Mediterranean world, arrive in concert at the conviction that Jesus was a unique and saving Son of God?"[256] The New Testament accounts describe the complete Christ-event as occurring historically in a particular place and time and make faith central to the impact of Jesus on his followers. Thus, it can be assumed that the flaw in Hick's perspective of

---

[255] James Edwards, *Is Jesus The Only Savior?* (Grand Rapids: William B. Eerdmans Publishing Company, 2005), 70.
[256] Ibid.

the historical Jesus originates in the interpretative methodology he uses to arrive at his conclusions. We must agree with Dunn that in the quest to find Jesus, the Jesus of history and the Jesus of faith must be viewed as one unit, or the real Jesus will never be found.

THE QUEST FOR HISTORICAL JESUS = THE JESUS OF HISTORY AND FAITH

HICK'S MISUSE OF FORM, SOURCE, AND REDACTION CRITICISM

Hick's basis for rejecting any passages referring to Jesus' deity or even to the primitive doctrines of high Christology is his belief that the Christ of faith was not a historical reality. Traditional Christians understand the New Testament documents as describing literal historical events. Hick, however, argues they are incomplete and obscure records of the "unknown man of Nazareth."[257] Hick asks, "Do we know enough about this Jesus whom we can be presenting to the world?"[258] Ironically, he can only declare that there is little to know about Jesus because he has stripped away all the layers of faith from the Christ of faith and from the Christ-events in the New Testament.

For Hick, it is essential that Jesus is not divine; thus, he has adopted a radical version of historical criticism and misused the tools of form and redaction criticism to fuel his false theories. He has adopted R. Bultmann's program of "demythologization" through which Bultmann attempted to separate what was historical from what was mythical in the biblical documents. Edwards explains, "Bultmann believed that the worldview of the New Testament was an obsolete one that had been replaced by modern science."[259] However, what Bultmann deems

---

[257] Hick, John, "Jesus and the World Religions," in *The Myth of God Incarnate*, (ed.) John Hick (London: SCM, 1977),167.

[258] John Hick, "What Does the Bible Really Say?" A sermon preached at Carrs Lane URC church, Birmingham, July 2005; available from http://www.johnhick.org.uk/; Internet; accessed November 18th, 2005.

[259] James Edwards, *Is Jesus The Only Savior?* (Grand Rapids: William B. Eerdmans Publishing Company, 2005), 27.

mythological or metaphorical is at the heart and soul of traditional Christianity; thus, Hick has been able to fit Bultmann's theories perfectly into his own pluralistic hypothesis.

It has been demonstrated that Hick incorporates radical form criticism. However, some would say that he and those before him have distorted the authentic process of this discipline. Form criticism is a method of examining forms of literature and "documents that preserve earlier tradition. Its basic assumption is that the earlier, oral use of the tradition shaped the material and resulted in the variety of literary forms found in the written record."[260] Conservative scholars such as James Dunn, Ronald Nash, Craig Blomberg, Donald Bloesch, and Stephen Evans would agree that the authentic process of the discipline has been abused by Hick and other liberal theologians he holds in high regard.

---

[260] Filson, Floyd V., "Form Criticism," in Lefferts A. Looetscher (ed.), *Twentieth Century Encyclopedia of Religious Knowledge. Vol.* 1 (Grand Rapids: Baker Book House, 1955), 436.

Source criticism is similar to form criticism. However, it differs in that it only examines literary sources for the life of Jesus written within ten to twenty years after the events of His life took place. Before the Christ-events were recorded in written form, they were preserved in an oral tradition. What form criticism attempts to accomplish is to fill in the gap between oral transmission and the written text. Form critics assume that the gospels were written in small separate units, which were independently circulated. Some critics believe, however, that over time these oral events took on "the form of various types of folk literature, such as legends, tales, myths, and parables."[261] Then, when a difficulty arose within the community, "they either created or preserved a saying or episode of Jesus to meet the needs of that particular problem."[262] Thus, some suggest that these sayings may not be a record of what actually occurred, but of beliefs and doctrines developed in the church over time. Based

---

[261] Joseph Fitzmyer, "Memory and Manuscript: The Origins and Transmission of the Gospel Tradition," *Theological Studies*, (September, 1962), 445.
[262] Ibid.

on this premise, radical liberals decide which events or units within the oral transmission were developed and which were historical.[263]

Some form critics also believe that the gospels were not written by the original authors but were later assembled by editors or redactors. Nash explains that redaction critics view these editors as being more than arrangers and compilers of original material, but also as theologians "whose arrangement of material was affected by their theological interests and their intentions."[264] Yet, even if there were additional writers involved in the process of composing the gospels, this possibility does not justify the assumption that they invented any passages or doctrines. One can easily identify the theological interests of the authors in every part of the New Testament; however, one need not necessarily conclude that all passages of faith have evolved from church doctrine as Hick claims. What solid piece of evidence does he have for

---

[263] Ibid.
[264] Ronald Nash, *Is Jesus the Only Savior?* (Grand Rapids: Zondervan Publishing House, 1994), 80.

making this assumption? Has he carefully considered the possibility that the theological content within the gospels and Paul's letters exists because they were historical accounts of the Christ-events? According to Nash, "It requires a whole set of additional presuppositions to conclude that the Evangelists produced only imaginative interpretations of Jesus with loose or even nonexistent historical ties."[265]

Josh McDowell warns that form criticism has gone too far, culminating in what is known as the Jesus Seminar, "eventually [becoming] more than a literary analysis. It developed into a historical analysis and began to pass judgment on the historicity of various passages of units."[266] It is obvious that there is a definite correlation between Hick's premise of graduated Christology within church history and the conclusions of the Jesus Seminar.

---

[265] Ibid.

[266] Josh McDowell, *The New Evidence That Demands a Verdict* (Nashville: Thomas Nelson Publishers, 1999), 562.

HICK'S GRADUATED CHRISTOLOGY AND

THE JESUS SEMINAR

The Jesus Seminar began as a reaction by the radical tradition (liberal theology) to the third quest for the historical Jesus. This third "new quest" was generated by biblical conservative scholars such as I. Howard Marshall, D. E. D. Moule, and R. Beasley-Murray, and also included scholars such as F. P. Sanders, Ben F. Meyer, Geza Vermes, Bruce Chilton, and James H. Charlesworth. Together, they rejected "the idea that the picture of the New Testament Jesus was somehow painted by Hellenic Savior cults" (Hick's belief).[267]

Scholars from the radical tradition are well represented in the Jesus Seminar, which was first organized in 1985 by Robert E. Funk. The seminar, first held in Santa Rosa, California, is ongoing. Up to seventy scholars meet together twice a year "to make pronouncements about

---

[267]Norman Geisler, *Baker Encyclopedia of Christian Apologetics* (Grand Rapids: Baker Books, 1998), 385.

the authenticity of the words and deeds of Christ."[268]
The seminar includes liberal Catholics, Protestants, Jews,
atheists, and many graduates from Harvard, Claremont,
or Vanderbilt Divinity Schools all strongly endorsed by
Hick as "theologically sound" educational institutions.
Using radical form criticism, the seminar committee
votes to decide which biblical words originated with
Jesus of Nazareth and which were created by church theology (faith).[269] The seminar has concluded that only
2 percent of what Jesus says in the New Testament can
be "absolutely regarded as His actual words. About 82
percent of what the canonical gospels ascribe to Jesus
is not authentic. Another 16 percent of the words are
of doubtful authenticity."[270] After this process of eliminating all faith elements, little of substance remains. Jesus
becomes hardly recognizable, transformed into a mere

[268] Ibid., 386.
[269] For more information regarding some major problems with the form critical method see Craig Blomberg, *The Historical Reliability of the Gospels*,
(Downers Grove: Inter-Varsity Press, 1987), 24-5.
[270] Josh McDowell, *The New Evidence That Demands a Verdict* (Nashville:
Thomas Nelson Publishers, 1999), 563.

man who taught peace and love, who never dreamed that He was God and who was, according to Hick, only a portal to the "Ultimate Real."

MAJOR FLAWS WITHIN THE JESUS SEMINAR'S CONCLUSIONS

Respected theologian James Dunn believes that the modern quests for historical Jesus, including the Jesus' seminars have focused too much attention on the literary culture, and thus arrived at a number of faulty conclusions regarding the Jesus traditions. He states the total impression left by Jesus has been subordinate to "fine-detailed critique and reconstruction without adequate appreciation of the extent to which that damaged the whole picture."[271] According to Dunn, these particular quests became a "rejection of the Gospels themselves

---

[271] James D. G. Dunn, *A New Perspective on Jesus: What the Quest for the Historical Jesus Missed* (Grand Rapids: Baker Academic, 2005), 46-7.

and their portrayal of Jesus and a deep seated suspicion of the Jesus tradition as a whole."[272]

The apostles, who were with Jesus day and night, did not change because they were in the presence of a representation of the "Ultimate Real." That kind of abstract encounter cannot change anyone. It is obvious that the main intent of the gospels is to preach salvation through Jesus' sacrifice on the cross and the power of His resurrection. Hick believes that the disciples created their faith theology of Jesus after His death and resurrection; however, they had been followers of Jesus long before the events of Easter. They had placed their faith in Jesus because, during their three years of interacting with Him, He made a lasting impression on their lives. Dunn believes that the disciple's "initial faith shaped the Jesus tradition from the first."[273]

The gospels reveal that as Jesus spoke with the authority of God, raising the dead, and commanding the

---

[272] Ibid., 22.
[273] Ibid., 24.

wind to stop and the demons to leave, information about Jesus rapidly spread throughout the country. Thus it is plausible to believe that the Jesus tradition began through verbal formulation "as the disciples talked together about the impact Jesus had made severally upon them."[274] This "verbal formulation" may have been a part of the Q source assumed to have shaped the gospel accounts or that the Q source may have been compiled after or even during the oral tradition. According to Dunn, the Q tradition[275] "reflects and bears testimony to the faith-creating impact of Jesus' ministry. It was formulated as an expression of faith, indeed, but of the faith of the disciples that drew them into following Him."[276] One can assume that much of what is contained in the gospels can be traced to the Jesus tradition of the early Twenties,

---

[274] Ibid., 27.

[275] The term "Q" comes from the German word "Quelle," or "source," and is assumed to have existed as a written or oral source used for teaching. It is also assumed that Matthew, and Luke used some of this unknown source to pen their accounts of Jesus. However, no one has actually seen Q and, thus, scholars cannot be sure whether it was a document, a source from the oral tradition, or both.

[276] James D. G. Dunn, *A New Perspective on Jesus: What the Quest for the Historical Jesus Missed* (Grand Rapids: Baker Academic, 2005), 28.

and Thirties, the historical period of Jesus' ministry. The contemporary obsession with Q has been influenced by a literary mind-set that assumes it was an actual Greek document containing many different layers developed through editing and redaction.[277] Although there is no conclusive evidence that such a manuscript ever existed, critics confidently refer to Q as an archeological artifact, assuming the existence of layers that can be removed to arrive at the original text. While the existence of an original source from which the gospel writers gathered their information is certainly within the range of possibility, it is also possible that Q never actually existed as a physical document. Dunn suggests that if we approach the Jesus tradition, even in its existing written form, as a variety of oral performances, "rather than edited versions of some 'original,' then our basic methodologies of source and form criticism become increasingly speculative in their application and uncertain in their outcome."[278]

[277] Ibid., 88.
[278] Ibid., 120.

In reality, one cannot strip away the traditional Christian perception of Jesus (faith) from tradition because this erasure leaves nothing of value. There is no historical Jesus to be found in the gospel records, "only the historic figure evident to us through the influence He exercised on His disciples, through the impact He made on them in calling them into discipleship."[279]

FINDING THE JESUS OF FAITH IN THE ORAL PROCESS

The oral tradition was recorded in Luke 1:1-4,

"Now many have undertaken to organize an account of the events fulfilled among us, just as they were handed down to us from the start by the eyewitnesses and reporters of the word. Therefore it seemed best to me also, because I have carefully

---

[279] Ibid.,33.

investigated everything from the beginning, to write for you an orderly record, most excellent Theophilus, so you may know for sure the truth of the words you have been taught." (Messianic Jewish Bible). Tree of Life Version (TLV).

As the disciples were with Jesus, they did not write books to keep the record of events. They had something much better - the oral tradition. The Jews believed that the traditions and teachings of the rabbis were to be something committed to the oral law and not something that was to be written down. It was to be passed down from teacher to disciple and they were responsible to accurately pass that information on to the next generation. The disciples would put to memory all the explanations, interpretations and even the stories, parables, illustrations and exegesis of the Scriptures which they were given. The disciples had their own disciples who "taught their disciples in the name of their own teacher, and his teacher and his teacher's teacher...transmitting a body of oral tradition as vast as the sea. This was a method of higher, religious education in the days of Yeshua."[280] The apostle Paul revealed his training when he gave his instructions to Timothy who was a Hellenistic Jew born of a Greek father: "The things which you have heard from me in the presence of many witnesses, entrust these to faithful men who will be able to teach others" (2 Timothy 2:2). We must understand that the process of the oral tradition was very disciplined and could even be more accurate than the written word. The Babylonian Talmud provides us with an example of the strict process the disciples undertook to pass on information orally. "The disciple who repeats his lesson one hundred times is not as worthy as the one who repeats his lesson one hundred and one times."[281]

According to Dunn, another flaw in the quest for historical Jesus is that our "ability to envisage the

---

[280] D. Thomas Lancaster, *Chronicles of the Messiah Book 1*, (Marshfield, MO, First Fruits of Zion, 2014), Introduction vi.

[281] Babylonian Talmud, (b. Chagigah 9b).

transmission of the Jesus Tradition [is] tightly constricted by the literary paradigm inbred in us."[282] Thus, Hick is unwilling to even consider the possibility that the oral tradition may not have functioned in the same way as the literary tradition. In studying the oral tradition of other cultures, R. Finnegan has discovered that listening to an oral "performance is not like reading a literary text."[283] While reading a text, one can refer back to a previous page, make a copy, edit and revise, or even take the text along to read later. On the other hand, an oral performance is "evanescent. It is an event. It happens and then is gone. Oral tradition is not there for the auditor to check back a few pages, or to take away, or to edit and revise. It is not a thing, an artifact like a literary text."[284]

These oral qualities are precisely why the Jesus of Nazareth cannot be found by Hick and the Jesus seminar.

---

[282] James D. G. Dunn, *A New Perspective on Jesus: What the Quest for the Historical Jesus Missed* (Grand Rapids: Baker Academic, 2005), 42

[283] R. Finnegan, *Oral Literature in Africa* (Oxford: Clarendon, 1970).

[284] James D. G. Dunn, *A New Perspective on Jesus: What the Quest for the Historical Jesus Missed* (Grand Rapids: Baker Academic, 2005), 46-7.

Their failure to recognize that the oral tradition is vastly different from the literary tradition is enough cause to be suspicious of their biased conclusions. When the early Christians passed on the letters (epistles) of Paul within the church, it was most likely done through the oral tradition, by hearing and repeating rather than through reading an actual text. Dunn explains that before the Jesus-events were recorded in writing, the transmission of these events to the new churches came through oral "performance recollection and celebration of and instruction and reflection on the Jesus tradition already familiar to the disciple groups. And all this would happen in oral mode."[285] The oral tradition was communal in character, giving community members the opportunity to scrutinize what was being performed and to compare their sense of the accuracy of what was being presented. Dunn says that it is not a stretch to imagine the earliest groups of disciples "being reminded of something Jesus said or

---

[285] Ibid., 48.

did and being similarly sparked to recall other similar teachings or events in Jesus' mission."[286]

Within the community, were special guardians of the oral tradition whose primary responsibility was to ensure that what was being performed publicly was an accurate account of the events. In other words, this teacher, guardian, or protector of the community's history was the reference resource for the local "oral" library. This referencing process could be what Luke refers to in Acts 2:42, when he mentions that the apostles gave themselves over to "teaching," most likely referring to the oral teaching tradition of the church.

Dunn believes that when we begin to shift out of a literary thought process and enter "more into an oral mind-set, we may find we have an explanation for the Jesus tradition that is itself largely sufficient to explain the character of the Synoptic tradition."[287] The oral tradition implies the witnessing of an event by more than

---

[286] Ibid., 49.
[287] Ibid., 53.

one witness; therefore, an event would be recalled from different perspectives. This dynamic can account for the slight differences in the synoptic accounts and explain the apparent contradictions Hick identifies.

Blomberg provides evidence for the memorizing tradition through the arguments of Harold Riesenfeld who published a seminal article in 1953 called, "The Gospel Tradition and its Beginnings." According to Blomberg, Riesenfeld argues the correct semblance for comprehending the history of the oral tradition "behind the gospels was not the relatively fluid process of transmitting popular folk-tales, as the form critic has assumed, but the much more rigid patterns of memorization and paraphrase dominant in rabbinic circles."[288] Riesenfeld believed that it was highly plausible that Jesus had his disciples memorize His most important teachings and particular historical events of His life.[289]

---

[288] Craig Blomberg, *The Historical Reliability of the Gospels* (Downers Grove: Inter-Varsity Press, 1987), 25. From Riesenfeld's essays, "The Gospel Tradition" (Philadelphia: Fortress, 1970), 1-29.
[289] Ibid., 26.

Find the Jesus of Faith: Delete the "Default Setting"

Another reason Hick and the Jesus seminar have failed to find the historical Jesus (and thus have assumed a gradualistic Christology) is that they separate Jesus from His context. According to Dunn, they need instead to observe "both that which was characteristic of Jesus as a Jew and that which is characteristic of the Jesus tradition as it now stands." [290] Dunn comments that "the characteristic features running through and across the Jesus tradition give us a clear indication of the impression Jesus made on his disciples during His mission." [291] Yet Hick and the others continue to return to the same old "default setting" generated by the literary paradigm. Our culture automatically thinks in a literary mode. Today's modern societies are the offspring of Gutenberg and Caxton cultures formed by the book.

---

[290] Ibid., 68-9.
[291] Ibid., 77.

Dunn says, "Our everyday currency is the learned article and monograph. Libraries are our natural habitat."[292] It is obvious that our culture is bound within a literary paradigm and thus, we are "in no fit state to appreciate how a nonliterary culture, an oral culture, functions."[293] For this reason, Dunn believes that the only way to begin an honest and fair process of form criticism is for the scholar or theologian to alter his or her default setting from a literary mind-set to an oral one. The scholarly disciplines began to make great strides in the Renaissance period because of increased interest in the study of classical texts. It became very important to translate books from their original languages, and we are indebted to scholars such as Erasmus who translated the first Greek New Testament.[294] Thus, Dunn believes that the only way the process of form criticism can be honest and fair

---

[292] Ibid., 82.

[293] James D. G. Dunn, *A New Perspective on Jesus: What the Quest for the Historical Jesus Missed* (Grand Rapids: Baker Academic, 2005), 83.

[294] The first translation of the Greek New Testament was done in 1516 by the Dutch theologian, classical scholar and humanist Desiderius Erasmus. For more information see, Walter A. Elwell (ed.), *Evangelical Dictionary of Theology* (Grand Rapids: baker Academic, 2005), 85.

is for the scholar or theologian examining the biblical texts to shift his or her default setting from a literary mindset to an oral one. Of course, this does not mean that the literary disciplines are to be abandoned altogether. What is required is that scholars acknowledge they are functioning according to a "default" literary presupposition that automatically interferes with any attempt to understand an oral tradition.

While it is true that the creation of form criticism was an honest attempt by Bultmann, Schleiermacher, and Wellhausen to break from the literary mind-set in order "to study the history of the oral tradition behind the gospels,"[295] their efforts failed because "Bultmann could not escape from the literary default setting; he could not conceive of the process of transmission except in literary terms."[296] Bultmann inappropriately used a literary method to access the oral tradition, stripping away

---

[295] R. Bultmann & K. Kundisin, *Form Criticism* (New York: Harper Torchbook, 1962), 1.

[296] James D. G. Dunn, *A New Perspective on Jesus: What the Quest for the Historical Jesus Missed* (Grand Rapids: Baker Academic, 2005), 85.

layer upon layer of what he believed was the Hellenistic theology of the Christ-events.

Hick concurs with Bultmann's methodology because it suits his hypothesis and enables him to conclude that Jesus was not God/Truth but that His deification was a literary evolution influenced by Hellenism. However, in his quest to discover the real Jesus of Nazareth, Hick has become a victim of the same literary bias as his mentor Bultmann. In his book *The Oral and Written Gospel*, W. H. Kelber agrees with Dunn that a major paradigm shift from literary presuppositions to understanding the oral traditions must occur within the scholarly world. However, the author believes that any quest for Jesus, even if it is informed by an understanding of the literary and oral paradigm, must begin its process with both the Jesus of history and faith, or He will not be discovered. Kelber encourages scholars to develop an understanding of what it must have been like to live and work in an oral society. He affirms the need for New Testament scholars to break free "from the unconscious presuppositions that shape the very way we see the Synoptic Problem and envisage the early transmission or retelling of the Jesus tradition."[297]

We have observed some evidence that Q may very well exist in an oral form or at least a combination of oral and literary forms under the guidance of the Holy Spirit. Oral accounts of the Jesus tradition were known, memorized, and shared before Mark penned these performances in literary form. Mark did not have to track down the first apostles or search high and low for deteriorating pieces of parchment hidden away in a basement. He did not have to uncover some unknown or unused tradition in order to finally write it down. The Jesus tradition continued in an oral form long after Mark recorded it in writing, because most early believers were not literate nor was there yet any printing press. Thus, the biblical writers had to pay attention to the accuracy of their written record because of the large auditory

---

[297] W.H. Kelber, *The Oral and Written Gospel* (Philadelphia: Fortress, 1983; reprinted, Bloomington: Indiana University Press, 1996), xv-xvi.

audience functioning as a check and balance to ensure the accuracy of the account. Altering a story in this kind of environment would be next to impossible, and thus a methodology assuming a linear development having "layer upon layer; edition following edition, is no longer appropriate."[298] Once we pay careful attention to the oral character "of the early Jesus tradition, we have to give up the idea of a single original form from which all other versions of the tradition are to be derived, as though the 'authenticity' of a version depended on our stability to trace it back to the original."[299]

I have shown that the oral tradition was a living tradition that could not be altered or analyzed by literary critics or redactors. It was "not so much reserved as performed, and not so much read as heard. To treat it as a lifeless artifact, suitable for clinical dissection, is to lose it."[300] Although Hick may argue that once the oral tradition was transcribed it could have substantially differed

---

[298] Ibid., 123.
[299] Ibid.
[300] Ibid., 125.

from its original oral form, he lacks substantial evidence on which to base his theory. The oral tradition was a living performative tradition that cannot be altered or analyzed by literary critics or redactors.

From Hick's perspective, the "real historical" Jesus is an impotent, powerless human being who is not God incarnate, and, thus, did not come to save the world from sin. However, Hick's historical Jesus does not exist because He is totally different from the authoritative, resurrected Jesus seen in the gospel accounts. Dunn declares, "There is no Galilean Jesus available to us other than the one who left such a strong impression in and through the Jesus tradition."[301] This is the Jesus the world needs to encounter and the Jesus that philosophers, scholars, and theologians must seek to rediscover. Why does the "real" Jesus and therefore the Truth remain so elusive for Hick and the Jesus Seminars? Because Jesus can be found only in the gospels as He is presented as the living and exclusive God incarnate, the Jesus of the

---

[301] Ibid., 78.

resurrection, the Jesus of humanity's salvation, the Jesus of history and faith, the Jesus who is the personification of the Truth without an "s."

The question is, do you really want to know the Truth? Jesus said that if you honestly seek Him, you will find Him. Jesus says in (Matthew 7:7) "Keep on asking, and you will receive what you ask for. Keep on seeking, and you will find. Keep on knocking, and the door will be opened to you. For everyone who asks, receives. Everyone who seeks, finds. And to everyone who knocks, the door will be opened." So, if you knock on the door of Truth and Jesus answers it, will you choose to come in and become His friend or will you walk away with indifference? And, if you walk or run away, to where will you run?

SUMMARY AND CONCLUSION

JESUS THE INCARNATION OF GOD— TRUTH WITHOUT AN "S"

"In essence, postmodern pluralism (Truth 's') has uncovered an ideology that Karl Marx could have used to erode the message of the cross without forcing the religion of atheism on his people. If it continues to permeate global culture, Hick's "theology" of religion could ultimately convince a great many people to follow a lie with grave consequences."-Author

Th•omas

Doubting Thomas
- John 20.24-29

After Pentecost, *Thomas'* journeys took *him* to *Parthia*, Persia and India *where* he established many *churches*. It is said that he *brought* the Good News of *Christ* to the Malabar Coast *where*, to this day, there is a *large* native population who *call* themselves 'Christians *of* St. Thomas'. Thomas *is* recognized as the *founder* of their church. *Tradition* says that Thomas *was* speared to death near Madras, India in A.D. *72*.

CANADIAN
BIBLE
SOCIETY

10 Carnforth Road, Toronto, ON M4A 2S4
Tel: (416) 757-4171 • Fax: (416) 757-3376
1-800-465-2425 • donorenq@biblesociety.ca
www.biblesociety.ca

Thomas

Thomas, also called Didymus (Greek for the 'twin'), is the disciple who is best known for his role in verifying the Resurrection. He was unwilling to believe that the other disciples had seen the risen Christ on the first Easter. He wanted to see and touch His wounds. When Christ appeared to the disciples eight days later, Thomas was shown the evidence he demanded. His scepticism gave rise to the modern day expression 'Doubting Thomas'.

CANADIAN BIBLE SOCIETY

SUMMARY AND CONCLUSION

This book has attempted to show evidence of traditional Christianity's belief in absolute Truth - the Truth being that Jesus is the physical revelation of God through the incarnation, despite the claims of John Hick's pluralistic hypothesis. In contrast to Hick's pluralism, the traditional Christian belief in Jesus' exclusive incarnation is not based on a hypothesis but on the foundation of personal testimony and the creeds of the oral tradition. Michel Schulz declares that "personal testimony is the most intense form of Truth. The category of testimony, which is the lifeblood of Christian theology, thus receives a further proof of its universal communicability and validity."[302]

The introduction concluded that in Hick's pluralistic theology of world religions, he successfully articulates in philosophical terms an ideology adopted culturally by Western society. Ironically, while the world's religions are not adopting Hick's "theological" theories of pluralistic religion, secular society and radical Western liberal theologians have embraced his revisionist perspective. It is the opinion of Catholic scholar Massimo Serretti that the "method and content of the pluralist theologies are meant to be the heart of what is in effect a new ideology, the suprareligious, in other words 'theological,' form of a new religious consciousness."[303] The pluralist motto is "the dissolution of religion as an original fact

---

[302] Schulz, Michael, "The Crux of the Pluralists: There is Only One God—Is There One Mediator?" in Massimo Serretti (ed.), *The Uniqueness and Universality of Jesus Christ: In Dialogue with the Religions*" (Grand Rapids: William B. Eerdmans Publishing Company, 2001), 132.

[303] Serretti, Massimo, "Theologies of Religious Pluralism" in Massimo Serretti (ed.), *The Uniqueness and Universality of Jesus Christ* (Grand Rapids: William B. Eerdmans Publishing Company, 2001), 101.

of man's creaturely condition into the 'religions.' "[304] In essence, postmodern pluralism (Truth 's') has uncovered an ideology that Karl Marx could have used to erode the message of the cross without forcing the religion of atheism on his people. If it continues to permeate global culture, Hick's "theology" of religion could ultimately convince a great many people to follow a lie with grave consequences. As Serretti asserts, "The ideology underlying the 'theologies' of religion is thus more subtle and destructive than open atheism, regardless of the pluralists' protestations to the contrary."[305]

Chapter one was the foundation on which I based my response to John Hick's pluralistic argument against my premise that Jesus Christ is the Truth personified and thus is the only way to forgiveness of sins and salvation. I defined some theological phrases and words in order for the reader to have a clearer understanding of my response to the assertions of relative pluralism. I also provided a

---

[304] Ibid., 101.
[305] Ibid.

foundation for absolute Truth as the primary evidence which solves the so called problem of evil.

I began chapter two describing why I chose John Hick as the pluralist to rebut in this study of Truth. We concluded that his move towards a pluralistic hypothesis was, in part, due to the influence of Immanuel Kant and Rudolph Bultmann. We learned what led to his decision to move from a Christocentric exclusive worldview to a pluralistic understanding of world religions. I revealed in his own words why he felt he could no longer believe that Jesus is the personification of Truth (God incarnate).

Chapter three began with a brief look at the two stages of Hick's pluralistic hypothesis - the progressive movement from a theocentric God model to an Unknowable Real salvation/liberation model. In contrast, traditional Christianity believes that God is a personal being who revealed Himself to humanity by coming to earth in human form as God incarnate. Hick totally denies the traditional Christian view of God's revelation and Jesus' incarnation, because it is incompatible with his hypothesis.

To believe it is to admit Christianity is the only Truth. Although Hick originally held a Christocentric model, he moved on to create a theocentric model, asserting that Christianity in particular needed to abandon its exclusivist deity theology. However, over time Hick discovered that his theocentric model of God was too Western in character and altered it to accommodate Eastern faiths that conceptualize God as a non-being that is totally transcendent and beyond human understanding.

Thus, Hick moved to embrace a more encompassing concept, that of the unknowable "Real" that he claims is inherent in all religions containing a salvation/ liberation belief system. In order for his pluralistic theories to be globally plausible, Hick needed a concept of god capable of incorporating both Eastern and Western views. However, Hick's new concept of the impersonal "Ultimate Real" resembles much more the unknowable transcendent entity of Eastern Religions, which can only be described by what it is not, than any Western concept of a personal deity. Although professing an inclusive religious pluralism, ultimately Hick creates an exclusivist pluralism that is intolerant of dissenting perspectives, thus contradicting his own ideology of tolerance. In addition, his concept of the unknowable "Real" contains many epistemological inconsistencies. If the "Real" is truly unknowable, one cannot know anything about it at all, yet Hick knows in some detail what it is not. Also, his assumptions about the "Real" are contradictory because an unknowable entity cannot be personal and impersonal, good and evil at the same time.

Chapter four revealed that because Hick's whole theory collapses if the incarnation is literal, he attempts to disprove the authenticity of the gospels, which in turn would discredit the deity of Jesus. Carruthers states that Hick's arguments against high Christology are outdated because "his theology is uncritically grounded in principles and attitudes of the late nineteenth century."[306] Hick

---

[306] Gregory H. Carruthers, S. J., The Uniqueness of Jesus Christ in the Theocentric Model of the Christian Theology of World Religions: An Elaboration and Evaluation of the Position of John Hick (Lanham: University Press of America, Inc., 1990), 329.

seems to lack awareness of recent scholarly research examining the oral tradition or the findings of the quest for the Jesus of history and faith undertaken by theologians such as Dunn, Blomberg, Bloesch, and Evans. Hick admits that most of his theoretical approach to Christology is borrowed from Schleiermacher and that his religious interpretation of religion comes primarily from Ludwig Feuerbach. In addition, "for his critique of Nicaea and his account of the origin of the doctrine of the Incarnation, Hick merely restates the turn-of-the-century thought of Adolf Harnack."[307]

For Hick, belief in the incarnation (the doctrine on which all other traditional Christian theologies rely) poses the greatest threat to his hypothesis. Therefore, not surprisingly, his first primary objection to incarnational theology focuses on discrediting or denying what Jesus claimed and knew about Himself. His second major argument, building on the first, casts doubt on the testimony of the early church witnesses in order to challenge

---

[307] Ibid., 330.

the authenticity of the gospel writers. If Hick can show that the church created the deity doctrine over time, then the gospel writers cannot be trusted. Hick's denial of Jesus' miracles and His resurrection as well as his rejection of the possibility of eyewitness testimonies to these events is based on his belief that high Christology was gradually developed by the church.

Chapter five focused on evidence that the early church showed a clear understanding and practice of high Christology, thus further weakening Hick's argument against the deity of Jesus and a gradualistic Christology. For belief in the incarnation of Jesus to be warranted, there must be historical evidence demonstrating that the apostles and early church believers (often martyrs) worshipped Jesus from the beginning. The passages affirming high Christocentric theology within the gospels, and especially in John's gospel, reveal what the early church believed and practiced even prior to the existence of any written records. Early creeds written in hymnal and poetic forms reveal that the early

Christians from the time of Jesus on were already memorizing and orally transmitting the Christ-events. From the very beginning, the oral tradition demonstrated a clear understanding of an incarnational doctrine.

Historical evidence paints a different picture than Hick presents in his hypothesis. Historical records show an early worship of Jesus, an early teaching of deity, and a common acceptance of the resurrection as a fact. Historical records have also demonstrated the transforming power of the Christ events on those who believed, even unto the death. The disciples were so greatly impacted by Jesus' teaching and His exclusive message of salvation for the world that His message became their motivation for preaching the gospel. The disciples and those who followed their teaching recognized that Jesus was no ordinary man. The early church fathers continued to maturate in their understanding of Jesus' deity, but stayed true to the teaching of the apostles. Even without other supporting evidence, the historical evidence presented in Chapter five is sufficient to warrant continued belief that Jesus Christ is the Truth personified.

Chapter six provides additional evidence and convincing arguments against Hick's two primary objections to the deity of Jesus. The author provides substantial evidence that Jesus' self-consciousness about His own deity was demonstrated through His God-like actions and authoritative teachings. Eyewitnesses experienced evidence of His authority over sin, sickness, death, nature, and the spirit world. In addition, Jesus' final shout to the world, through His own resurrection, revealed His authority over death. While the early eyewitnesses to the Christ-events may not have been able to fully understand or explain how the incarnation was possible, in time the church was forced to not only more fully explain Jesus' incarnation but also to defend this doctrine against those who would corrupt the Truth.

Jesus did not say the words, "I am God Incarnate;" however, His claim to deity was clear by His Words, teaching, and actions throughout His life. There is ample evidence that those who witnessed his life noticed these clues and concluded that He was God incarnate. Unfortunately, Hick will not allow history to speak, even when there is a myriad of witnesses waiting to verify the facts of the gospels. Carruthers aptly comments that, "by being made 'Lord' of history upon His resurrection, it is no longer history which contains Jesus, but it is the risen Jesus who contains history."[308]

Hick's second primary objection, building on his premise that Jesus did not claim His own deity, is that the high Christology within the New Testament cannot have been part of the original text but must have been developed later. Hick argues that the early church gradually created the deity doctrine, generating the resurrection story, which the gospel writers recorded sixty or seventy years later. However, Hick cannot explain away the existing eyewitness accounts of Jesus life, death, and resurrection that must be believed unless there are good reasons to distrust this historical testimony. These

---

[308] Ibid., 313.

accounts must be considered reliable unless Hick has another five hundred witnesses to counter the claims of the five hundred or more that testified to Jesus' post-resurrection appearances. Yet Hick refuses to follow the principle of credulity, which is a basic rational principle. Unless Hick can show equal counter evidence to the Christ-events and provide convincing reasons for doubting the gospel narratives, "wholesale a priori skepticism is unjustified."[309] Paul's letters could have been written as early as five to ten years after the resurrection, and the gospel accounts as early as thirty to fifty years later. Accounts of the Christ-events were compiled by the gospel writers from a combination of oral eyewitness accounts and from a variety of carefully written documents. Thus, Evans declares, "It is therefore a certainty that positive historical testimony exists for the Incarnational narrative."[310]

---

[309] Stephen Evans, *The Historical Christ and the Jesus of Faith: The Incarnational Narrative as History* (Oxford: Clarendon Press, 1996), 335.
[310] Ibid., 336.

Chapter seven presented some of the most significant evidence supporting warranted belief that Jesus was the incarnation of God and closed with one final argument regarding the oral tradition. I examined James Dunn's short but eye-opening book, *A New Perspective on Jesus*, where he identifies a number of primary errors made by scholars questing to discover the historical Jesus. His theory is that the truth about Jesus has remained hidden from liberal Western scholars and theologians "because they started from the wrong place, from the wrong assumptions, and viewed the relevant data from the wrong perspective."[311] I believe that if these incorrect assumptions can be corrected, modern scholars may be at a portal that could reveal a new understanding of the oral traditions' affirmation of incarnational theology.

The first error Hick and other liberal theologians holding the same presuppositions continue to make, according to Dunn, is "to assume that faith is a hindrance

---

[311] James D. G. Dunn, A New Perspective on Jesus: What the Quest for the Historical Jesus Missed (Grand Rapids: Baker Academic, 2005), 15.

to the quest, something that had to be stripped away if the quester was to gain a clear view of the historical Jesus."[312] Instead, the starting point of any quest for the historical Jesus needs to begin with the historical fact that Jesus made a major faith impact on His disciples.

Dunn asserts that the second mistake made by liberal scholars is the assumption that we can effectively understand the Jesus tradition by examining it solely through the lens of the literary paradigm. If Hick would remove the literary blinders or default settings that have been permanently etched on all modern minds and start to investigate how the Jesus tradition functioned in the oral period of church history, he might begin to discover the real Jesus.

Hick's third error is to impose an interpretative dissimilation methodology that operates on the assumption that it is possible to distinguish the Christ-events that actually happened from those that were created over time. Yet, one must ask if it is possible to distinguish the

---

[312] Ibid., 57.

historical event from the theological event. Hick does not even consider the possibility that a theological belief can be intertwined within a historical event. It makes no sense to distinguish Jesus from His context. Rather, one must search for the "characteristic Jesus, both that which was characteristic of Jesus as a Jew and which is characteristic of the Jesus tradition as it now stands."[313] James Dunn has begun to explore what may become an important theological breakthrough in finally resolving the futile quest for the historical Jesus. He has confronted scholars with the need to gather new evidence from the oral tradition and to study the Scriptures from the perspective of an oral mindset as well as from a critical literary perspective. This new approach has the potential to create another Copernican revolution where the world discovers Jesus as Truth, and at the center of His creation and as the only revelation of God sacrificed for the salvation of all humanity. Hick and other radical liberal theologians and philosophers have far too long avoided

---

[313] Ibid., 69.

the eyewitness support for deity theology presented by the apostles who were influenced and changed by the extraordinary claims of the God/man Jesus.

The Christian faith rests on a revelation that took place in and through the historical life, death, and resurrection of Jesus of Nazareth. 'This full Christ-event already contained the truth of its meaning, a meaning that would be affirmed in faith and developed in theology. It is for this reason that the language of Jesus' incarnation is not mythological, and that it does affirm the objective truth about the uniqueness of Jesus as the world's Savior.'[314]

Chapter 8 concluded with a resolve that Jesus is the Truth with a capital "T" and that there cannot be multiple truths because then reality rests on a crumbling foundation. The evidence that I have presented here has conclusively established warranted belief in the revelation

---

[314] Gregory H. Carruthers, S. J., *The Uniqueness of Jesus Christ in the Theocentric Model of the Christian Theology of World Religions: An Elaboration and Evaluation of the Position of John Hick* (London: University Press of America, 1990), 298.

of God to the world, through the exclusive incarnation of Jesus Christ. The church has held this doctrine for more than two thousand years and will continue this affirmation until the return of our Lord. The search for the true identity of Jesus will end only with the acknowledgment that God has revealed Himself in Jesus as the Truth. Bloesch declares, "Our faith is not in the Jesus of history or in the eternal Christ but in the historical Jesus Christ, who was both fully divine and fully human at the same time."[315] Thus Hick's pluralistic hypothesis will need someone to develop additional stages and new epicycles if it is to retain any future following.

What must the church do in the face of John Hick's truth with an "s" hypothesis? Should one withdraw from culture and retreat into the church, setting up walls of defense to be insulated from a world that has no tolerance for those who believe in the exclusivity of their faith? No! The response must be the same as it was when

---

[315] Donald Bloesch, *Jesus Christ: Savior and Lord* (Downers Grove: Inter-Varsity Press, 1997), 72.

the early church encountered its world of pluralism, to go into all the world and show them the only way home - Jesus, the Way, the Truth, and the Life. "For God so loved the world, that He gave His only begotten Son, that whosoever believes in Him shall not perish but have eternal life. For God did not send the Son into the world to judge the world, but that the world might be saved through Him" (John 3:16-17). Martin Luther was a strong defender of absolute Truth and stated, "Take away assertions and you take away Christianity. The truths that he burns on our hearts are twice as inflexible as the Stoics. The Holy Spirit is no skeptic."[316] I believe that if we do not preach salvation in Jesus only, we will also have to stand judged and guilty before the throne of God. The contemporary church in the West must make a choice to live in the power of the living Christ or retreat into the contradicting, powerless, confusing labyrinth of pluralism. "Either we 'keep faith with Darwin' and

[316]Martin Luther, The Bondage of the Will, trans. Henry Cole (Grand Rapids, Mich.: Eerdmans, 1931), p. 24.

embrace postmodernism, or we keep faith with a personal God who is not silent—whose Logos is the source of unified, universal, capital-T Truth."[317]

It is my sincere prayer that the evidence presented in this book may save many from falling into the false pit of John Hick's exclusive pluralism. My heart is torn when I observe those who say they are followers of Jesus, and then turn away from the only Truth which is able to bring a fallen humanity back into the garden. Apologist Nancy Pearcey believes the church is in a battle that it will win in the end, but it will not be easy. She says, "In order to communicate the gospel in the West, we face a unique challenge: We need to learn how to liberate it from the private sphere and present it in its glorious fullness as the truth about all reality."[318] Jesus refers to Himself in Revelation 1:8 as "...the Alpha and the Omega--the beginning and the end..."I am the one who is, who always was, and who is still to come

---

[317] Nancy Pearcey, *Total Truth: Liberating Christianity from Its Cultural Captivity,*
[318] Ibid, chapter 2

- the Almighty One." Humanity will find the peace that passes all understanding only when it realizes, understands, repents and then chooses to have a personal relationship with Jesus. In CE 449, Pope Leo proclaimed that "our faith will finally be defended to good purpose when the false opinion is condemned even by its adherents."[319] In the end, the meaning and work of the cross will triumph over those who oppose it, and all the world will bow before the TRUTH—JESUS!

TRUTH IS NOT PLURAL !

---

[319] "Pope Leo 1's Letter to Flavian of Constantinople," in *The Christological Controversy* (ed.) Richard A. Norris, Jr. (Philadelphia: Fortress, 1980), 155.

SCRIPTURE REFERENCES

Preface

John 8:31-32

John 8:44

Philippians 2:9-11

Chapter one

John 10:30

John 14:9b

John 14: 6

1 John 4:9-10

Proverbs 14:12

Chapter two

2 Corinthians 7:9-10

Chapter three

Romans 1:18-21

Colossians 2:8

John 14:6

Colossians 1:15

Titus 2:11

Chapter Four

John 14:6

Acts 2:22

Mark 1:1

Luke 3:28

Luke 20:36

Chapter Five

John 1:1

Genesis 1:1

John 1:3

John 1:14

John 1:5-11

John 1:9, 29

John 3:16-18

John 5:18

John 1:2, 8:23, 8:58, 16:27-28

John 8:58

John 10:28-30

John 14:6

John 17:5, 24

John 17:3

John 19:7; 10:36

John 20:28

Mark 1:2-3

Matthew 1:21, 23

Matthew 2:11

Matthew 13:9

Matthew 28:9,17

Matthew 11:27

Matthew 24:14

Matthew 28:19-20

Acts 4:12

Luke 24:51-52

Luke 10:1

Romans 16:23

Acts 19:29

Acts 21:29

Acts 1:23

Acts 9:10

I Corinthians 16:22

Romans 1:3-4

1 Corinthians 11:23ff

Philippians 2:6-11

Colossians 1:15-18

1 Timothy 3:16

1 Corinthians 15:3-8

Acts 18, 19, and 20

Galatians 1:18-19

Acts 9:20

1Timothy 3:16

Chapter Six

1 Timothy 2:5-6

Matthew 11:4

John 10:36; 19:7

Matthew 27:43

Mark 1:22

Mark 2:27-28

Mark 1:21-28; 3:1-6

John 9:14

Mark 1:24; 3:11; Luke 4:41

Mark 5:7

Matthew 8:2-4

Mark 1:40-45

Luke 5:12-16

Matthew 9:18-26

Mark 5:21

John 6:40, 44, 54

Matthew 8:23-27;

Mark 4:35

Matthew 14:25

Mark 6:30

Roman 3:23

1 John 1:9

Luke 5:21

Matthew 9:6

Peter 1:19; 2:22

1 Corinthians 5:21

John 8:46

1 John 4:2

John 3:3-5

1 Timothy 4:20, 6:3;

2 Corinthians 11:13

Galatians 2:4

2 Peter 2:1

Matthew 26:63

Mark 14: 60-62

Luke 1:32-35

Matthew 4:3,6

Mark 3:11

Matthew 16:16

Chapter 7

Acts 9:27,28

1 Corinthians 15:1-7

1 John 1:1-5

Luke 1:1-4

2 Timothy 2:2

Acts 2:42

Matthew 7:7

Chapter 8

Acts 9:27,28

John 3:16-17

Revelation 1:8

John 3:16-17

SELECTED
BIBLIOGRAPHY

Anderson, Sir Norman. *Christianity and World Religions: The Challenge of Pluralism.* Downers Grove: Inter-Varsity Press, 1984.

Aquinas, Thomas. *Summa Theologica.* II/II, Q.1, art.2.

Augustine: Augustine, *Treatises on Various Subjects,* Edited by Roy J. Deferrari, Catholic University of America Press, INC., Washington, D.C. 1952, 78.

Barth, Karl. *Church Dogmatics.* Translated by T.H.L. Parker et al., ed. G. W. Bromley and T. F. Torrance. Edinburgh: T. & T. Clark, 1957.

Bettenson, Henry, ed. Documents of the Christian Church. New York: Oxford University Press, 1981.

Bloesch, Donald G. *God the Almighty, Power, Wisdom, Holiness, Love.* Downers Grove: Inter- Varsity Press, 1995.

_____. *Jesus Christ: Savior and Lord.* Downers Grover: Inter-Varsity Press, 1997.

Blomberg, Craig. *The Historical Reliability of the Gospels.* Dowers Grove: Inter-Varsity Press, 1987.

_____. *The Historical Reliability of John's Gospel: Issues & Commentary.* Dowers Grove: Inter-Varsity Press, 2001.

Bultmann, R. & K., Kundisin. *Form Criticism.* New York: Harper Torchbook, 1962.

Burridge, Richard and Graham, Gould. *Jesus Now and Then.* Grand Rapids: William B. Eerdmans Publishing Company, 2004.

Bush, Russ, ed. Classical Readings in Christian Apologetics: AD 100-1800. Grand Rapids: Baker Books, 1996.

Byron, William, ed. "Foxe's Book of Martyrs." Available from, www.sacred-texts.com/chr/martyrs.fox101.htm; Internet; accessed September 4, 2006.

Carey, L.G. "Justin Martyr." *The New International Dictionary of the Christian Church*. Apology 1:21-33; Dialogue with Trypho the Jew. Revised, J.D. Douglas., ed., Michigan: Grand Rapids, Zondervan, 1978.

Carruthers, S. J., Gregory H. The Uniqueness of Jesus Christ in the Theocentric Model of the Christian Theology of World Religions: An Elaboration and Evaluation of the Position of John Hick. Lanham: University Press of America, Inc., 1990.

Carson, D.A. *The Gagging of God: Christianity Confronts Pluralism*. Zondervan, Grand Rapids, Michigan, 1996.

CNN News, Available from, https://en.oxforddictionaries.com/word-of-the-year-2016, Internet; accessed November 18, 2016.

Confident Christians, *http://confidentchristians.org*, Internet; accessed February 7, 2017.

Craig, William L. Reasonable Faith: Christian Truth and Apologetics. Wheaten: Moody Press, 1984.

_____. "No Other Name: A Middle Knowledge Perspective on the Exclusivity of Salvation Through Christ." *Faith and Philosophy* 6 (1989).

Cramer, David. *Internet Encyclopedia of Philosophy*, http://www.iep.utm.edu/hick/, Accessed March 8, 2017.

D'Costa, Gavin. "Revelation and World Religions." In Paul Avis, ed. *Divine Revelation*. Grand Rapids: W. B. Eerdmans Publishing Company, 1997.

_____. Theology and Religious Pluralism, the Challenge of Other Religions. Oxford: Basil Blackwell Ltd, 1996.

Doyle, Sir Arthur Conan. *Sherlock Holmes in: The Sign of the Four*, Doubleday 1890.

Dunn, James. *Christology in the Making: A New Testament Inquiry into the Origins of the Doctrine of the Incarnation.* London: SCM, 1980.

_____. *A New Perspective on Jesus: What the Quest for the Historical Jesus Missed.* Grand Rapids: Baker Academic, 2005.

_____. *The Evidence for Jesus.* Philadelphia: The Westminster Press, 1985.

Edwards, James R. *Is Jesus the Only Savior?* Grand Rapids: William B. Eerdmans Publishing Company, 2005.

Elwell, Walter A., ed. *Evangelical Dictionary of Theology.* Grand Rapids: Baker Book House, 1984.

Evans, C. Stephen. The Historical Christ and the Jesus of Faith: The Incarnational Narrative as History. Oxford: Clarendon Press, 1996.

Filson, Floyd V. "Form Criticism." *In Twentieth Century Encyclopedia of Religious Knowledge*, ed, Lefferts A. Looetscher Vol. 1. Grand Rapids: Baker Book House, 1955.

Finnegan, R. *Oral Literature in Africa*. Oxford: Clarendon, 1970.

Fitzmyer, Joseph. "Memory and Manuscript: The Origins and Transmission of the Gospel Tradition." *Theological Studies*. Vol. 23. (September 1962)

Geisler, Norman L. *Baker Encyclopedia of Christian Apologetics*. Grand Rapids: Baker, 1998.

Geisler, N. L., and P. K, Hoffman. *Why I Am a Christian: Leading Thinkers Explain Why They Believe*. Grand Rapids: Baker Books, 2001.

Geivett, Douglas R. *"Is Jesus the Only Way?"* In *Jesus Under Fire*. Michael, eds. J. Wilkins and J. P. Moreland, Grand Rapids: Zondervan Publishing House, 1995.

Green, Keith Gordon / Melody, *No One Believes In Me Anymore,* lyrics © 1977, Sony/ATV Music Publishing LLC.

Green, Michael. *But Don't All Religions Lead to God?* Grand Rapids: Baker Books, 2002.

Habermas, Gary R. *The Historical Jesus: Ancient Evidence for the Life of Jesus.* Nashville: Thomas Nelson Publishers, 1994.

Hengel, Martin. *Between Jesus and Paul.* Philadelphia: Fortress, 1983.

Hick, John. "A Pluralist View." In *Four Views: Salvation in a Pluralistic World,* eds. Dennis L. Okholm and Timothy R. Phillips, Grand Rapids: Zondervan Publishing House, 1996.

_____. *An Autobiography,* Oneworld Plublications, 185 Banbury Road, Oxford OX2 7AR, England, 2002.

_____. *An Interpretation of Religion: Human Responses to the Transcendent.* New Haven: Yale University Press/Macmillan Press Ltd., 1989.

_____. *Disputed Questions in Theology and the Philosophy of Religion.* New Haven: Yale University Press/Macmillan Press Ltd., 1993.

_____. *God and the Universe of Faiths.* London: Macmillan Press Ltd., 1973.

_____. *God Has Many Names*. Philadelphia: Westminster, 1982.

_____. "Jesus and the World Religions." *In The Myth of God Incarnate*, ed., John Hick, London: SCM, 1977.

_____. *The Metaphor of God Incarnate*. Louisville: John Knox Press, 1993.

_____. "The Non-Absolutism of Christianity." In *The Myth of Christian Uniqueness*, eds. John Hick and Paul F. Knitter, New York: Orbis Books, 1987.

_____. *The Rainbow of Faiths: A Christian Theology of Religions*. Louisville: John Knox Press, 1995.

_____. "The Theology of Pluralism." *Theology* 86 (1993).

_____. "What Does the Bible Really Say?" Available from http://www.johnhick.org.uk/; Internet; accessed; 25 October, 2005.

Hunter, A. M. *Jesus Lord and Savior*. Grand Rapids: Eerdmans, 1976.

Kasper, Walter Cardinal. "The Uniqueness and Universality of Jesus Christ." In *The Uniqueness and Universality of Jesus Christ: In Dialogue with the Religions* ed. Massimo Serretti, Grand Rapids: Eerdmans Publishing Company, 2004.

Keffer Lindy, http://www.focusonthefamily.com/parenting/teens/absolute-truth, Internet; Accessed January 30, 2017. Copyright © 2000 Focus on the Family, Originally titled "*Ultimate Truth: Discovering Absolutes in a 'Whatever' World.*"

Kelber, W.H. The Oral and Written Gospel. Philadelphia: Fortress, 1983; reprinted, Bloomington: Indiana University Press, 1996.

Keyes, Ralph. *The Post-Truth Era: Dishonesty and Deception in Contemporary Life.* St. Martin's Press, New York, 2004.

Knight, George A. F. *I Am, This is My Name: The God of the Bible and the Religions of Man.* Grand Rapids: Eerdmans Press, 1993.

Lewis, C. S. *The Weight of Glory and Other Addresses*, Rev. exp. New York: Macmillian, 1980.

_____. *Mere Christianity*. HarperSanFrancisco, Zondervan Publishing House,1952.

Lancaster, Thomas D. *Chronicles of the Messiah, Book 1*. (Marshfield, MO, First Fruits of Zion, 2014), Introduction vi.

Lightfoot, J. B. and Harmer, J. R. *Apostolic Times.* Grand Rapids: Baker Book House, 1998.

Lindsley, Art. *True Truth: Defending Absolute Truth in a Relativistic World* (Kindle Locations (197-199). Kindle Edition.

Luther, Martin. *The Bondage of the Will*, trans. Henry Cole (Grand Rapids, Mich.: Eerdmans, 1931), p. 24.

Lonergan, Bernard. *The Way to Nicaea: The Dialectical Development of Trinitarian Theology*. London: Dalton, Longman & Todd, 1976.

Marshall, Howard I. "Incarnational Christology in the New Testament." *In Christ the Lord*, ed. H. H. Rowdon. Leicester: Inter-Varsity Press, 1982.

McDowell, Josh. *The New Evidence that Demands a Verdict.* Nashville: Thomas Nelson Publishers, 1999.

Menke, Karl-Heinz. "Jesus Christ: The Absolute in History? The Question Concerning the Universal Significance of a Historical Fact." In *The Uniqueness and Universality of Jesus Christ,* ed.

Massimo Serretti. Grand Rapids: Eerdmans Publishing Company, 2001.

Montgomery, John Warwick. *The Shape of the Past.* Ann Arbor: Edwards Brothers, 1962. Moreland, J. P. *Scaling the Secular City.* Grand Rapids: Baker Book House, 1987.

Morris, Leon. *The New International Commentary on the New Testament: The Gospel According to John.* Grand Rapids: William B. Eerdmans Publishing Company, 1989.

Moule, C. F. D. The Birth of the New Testament. Revised edition, New York: Harper and Row, 1982.

Moyer, Elgin. *Wycliffe Biographical Dictionary of the Church.* Grand Rapids: Baker Book House, 1998.

Muncaster, Ralph O. *Evidence for Jesus.* Eugene: Harvest House Publishers, 1984.

Nash, Ronald. *Is Jesus the Only Savior?* Grand Rapids: Zondervan Publishing House, 1994.

Netland, Harold. Dissonant Voices: Religious Pluralism and the Question of Truth. Grand Rapids: _____. *Encountering Religious Pluralism: The Challenge to Christian Faith and Mission.* Downers Grove: Inter-Varsity Press, 2001.

Newbigin, Lesslie. *The Gospel in a Pluralistic Society.* Grand Rapids: William B.Eerdmans Publishing Company, 1989.

O'Connor, Timothy. "Religious Pluralism." In *Reason for the Hope Within* ed. Michael Murray, Grand Rapids: William B. Eerdmans Publishing Company, 1999.

Packer, J. I, and Thomas C.Oden. *One Faith, The Evangelical Consensus.* Downers Grove: Inter-Varsity Press, 2004.

Pinnock, Clark H. "A Pluralist View: Response to John Hick." *In More Than One Way: Four Views on Salvation in a Pluralistic World* eds. Dennis L. Okholm & Timothy R. Phillips, Grand Rapids: Harper Collins Publishers, 1995.

_____. *Wideness in God's Mercy, the Finality of Jesus Christ in a World of Religions.* Grand Rapids: Zondervan Publishing House, 1992.

Plantinga, Alvin. *Warranted Christian Belief.* Oxford: Oxford University Press, 2000.

"Pope Leo 1's Letter to Flavian of Constantinople." In *The Christological Controversy,* ed. Richard A. Norris, Jr., Philadelphia: Fortress, 1980.

Rivero, Michael, "Hate Speech' And The massive Israeli US Spying Operation." Available from http://rense.

com/general24/spy.htm, Internet; accessed, January 6th 2016.

Sanders, E. P. *Jesus and Judaism.* London: SCM Press, 1985.

Schulz, Michael. "The Crux of the Pluralists: There is Only One God—Is there One Mediator?" *In The Uniqueness and Universality of Jesus Christ: In Dialogue with the Religions,* ed. Massimo Serretti. Grand Rapids: William B. Eerdmans Publishing Company, 2001.

Serretti, Massimo. "Theologies of Religious Pluralism." In *The Uniqueness and Universality of Jesus Christ,* ed. Massimo Serretti, Grand Rapids: William B. Eerdmans Publishing Company, 2001.

Schaeffer Francis, *The Evangelical Disaster*, Crossway Books, 1300 Crescent Street, Wheaton Illinois, 1984.

_____. Address given at the University of Notre Dame, 1981.

Shenk, Calvin E. *Who Do You Say that I Am? Christians Encounter Other Religions.* Scottdale: Herald Press, 1997.

Snodgrass, Klyne. *Between Two Truths - Living with Biblical Tensions,* 1990, Zondervan Publishing House, p. 35.

Spencer, Archie. "The Pluralist and Inclusivist Appeal to the Religious Sense as a Basis for Inter Religious Dialogue." *In God the Creator, Sustainer and Redeemer.* Appendix 2, Short Notes for Students, summer, 2005.

Stegemann, E.W, and W. Stegemann. *The Jesus Movement: A Social History of Its First Century.* Translated by O. C. Dean Jr. Minneapolis: Fortress Press, 1995.

Stetson, Brad. *Pluralism and Particularity in Religious Belief.* Westport: C.T. Preger Publishers, 1994.

Stevenson, J., ed. *A New Eusebu.* London: SPCK, 1998.

Strobel, Lee. *A Case For Faith: A Journalist Investigates the Toughest Questions of the Christian Faith*, Zondervan, Grand Rapids, Michigan, 2000. Quoting Ravi Zacharias, Jesus Among Other gods: The Absolute Claims of the Christian Message.

Turner, Steve. https://www.poemhunter.com/poem/creed/, Internet; Poem Hunter.com. Accessed March 7th, 2017, Copyright © 2003

Zacharias, Ravi. *Jesus Among Other Gods: The Absolute Claims of the Christian Message.* Nashville: W. Publishing Group, 2000.

_____, [What About the Foundation?, *"If the Foundations Be Destroyed,"* Preaching Today, Tape No. 142.]

Look for Conrad's Second Book

Coming Soon

STORY #1

"A MASTERPIECE" EVIDENCE OF BEAUTY AND DESIGN

PRELUDE

There was an eerie blue haze cast by a full moon over the calm waters of the Antarctic Ocean. All was quiet except for the lapping of water against the five million-mile sheet of ice covering the largest rock mass in the world. I turned my head from side to side looking for any sign of danger, not that it would do any good if a sperm whale thought I was a fillet fish sandwich. "I guess I'm the first one here as usual," I said to myself as the scent of fresh fish lured me under the frigid water for a hopeful look. Darting side to side, back and forth through the icy water like an Olympic bobsled speeding towards the finish line, I snagged the fish. Still moving at breath taking speeds I slid up through the surface of the water and landed with a twenty-foot slide onto the snow covered strata. Waddling towards a flat surfaced rock I sat down, swallowed the fish, shook the water off my back and drifted off to sleep. I was awakened by a thundering crash as a giant piece of melting ice slid into the water. The spray washed me back into the ocean and I was surprised by my two friends, Skeeter and Jack, who came up out of nowhere and simultaneously slapped me on the side of my head with their flippers.

"Hi Pete," they chirped, "We've been looking for you all night. Are you ready for our annual adventure in discussing another topic regarding the existence of God?" asked Jack as he shook the water out of his ears.

"What are we going to discuss this year, Jack?" asked Skeeter. "You're still not attempting to prove that you possess the exclusive truth that Jesus is the only way to God are you?"

CHAPTER 1

INTRODUCING THE THREE PHILOSOPHICAL PENGUINS

PETER FREEZEN - THE PLURALIST

(A Meddling Moderator)

"Hi, my given name is Pete, Pete the Penguin. My friends all call me Petra because I was actually born in the cold waters of the South Pole, and my egg was thought to have been frozen solid. It may seem somewhat strange but my family name is Freezen, (no pun intended). My two friends are Jack Frost and

Skeeter Froze. It looks like they're already at each other, which means it's going to be a lively discussion this year. We're known as "The Three Penguins," the only frozen philosophers of religion in the world – at least as far as I know. Every year we take a break from our busy schedules of fishing, being hunted, and hobnobbing with the social elite to meet somewhere in the world to discuss the existence of God.

"I would describe myself as somewhat short and skinny for a penguin. I'm always teased about wearing these huge horn rim glasses held together in the middle with black electrical tape and especially about my unusual birth. You see, my mom was one week from laying her first egg of the season and was fishing with her friends when I surprised everyone and as she says, "he just popped out!" I apparently drifted slowly to the bottom, and my mom instinctively dove down after me against the advice of all the other females. They told her that I would never hatch and that there would be many other eggs in the future. Being a preemie, my egg was smaller than usual and so mom picked me up with her flippers, tucked me into her soft downy feathers and headed for the surface. She made my dad keep me warm, and he became the laughing stock of all the males that year. They told him that the egg was frozen solid by now and he was wasting his time waiting for a miracle. Well here I am, a miracle. I'd say more of a fluke of nature, sickly, and a little small for my age but smart as a sea lion.

I guess you could say I'm a positively nerdy bird with a pluralistic bend. You see, I believe not only that everybody in the world has the right to believe what he or she wants to believe, but also that each belief is his or her truth. Jack and I are always arguing whether there is an absolute truth in the world or not. My truth is that God, (whoever each person equally believes that to be), has allowed man to find Him in many creative ways, which differ from culture to culture but which eventually leads directly to Him. I find Jack quite exclusive, arrogant and bigoted when he says Christianity is the only true religion. I believe everyone has a right to define the god of their own choosing even if it ends up to be themselves."

JACK FROST —THE JESUS FREAK
(A Fundamentalist Theologian)

Then, there is my best friend Jack, Jack Frost. He is what many of you humans would call a fundamentalist Christian (a Jesus freak) whose prime reality or worldview begins with a Master Creator of all things who has a plan and purpose for everyone. He believes that the Bible is God's Word, spoken through the personalities of the authors and inspired by the Holy Spirit. He believes that since the Bible is God's Word it contains the infallible, (without any mistakes) absolute truth. Jack has a strong belief in a finite universe that was caused by a Master Artist who carefully and methodically painted a world within this universe exclusively for humanity. Jack also believes that a relationship with Jesus is the only passageway to God and the only way to be "saved," whatever that means.

He's tall, has a full head of feathers, a big grin, and is somewhat good looking for a Northern bird from Argentina. He has a wife Jamie and two young chicks still in the nest that he calls his little burnt wieners, because when they were hatched their feathers were completely black. He says they are a special gift from God, however, I believe they're kind of freaks of nature, if you know what I mean. I believe 'normal' Penguins should not be exclusively black (not that there is anything wrong with that, however, they must have some white feathers too, that is just the way things are, right."

SKEETER FROZE – THE SKEPTIC
(A Bird with Issues)

"Skeeter Froze reads Shakespeare, has an over sized beak, large webbed feet and gray feathers. He likes to eat, so some might say he's horizontally challenged, yet a rather distinguished looking gentleman. He seems quite religious; however, he's not sure about anything right now. Skeeter would somewhat agree with me in that there is no one spiritual journey that leads to the truth, but than again what is truth? I would agree with my friend Skeeter, who believes the word "truth" to be a confusing word to define these days, since we would believe it to be relative to our cultural setting and the community we were raised."

"Hey Pete, are you done mumbling to yourself yet?" chirped Jack. "Let's get on with this, I don't have all week to win you both to Jesus you know, I have a wife and chicks waiting for me to come home."

CHAPTER 2

MYSTERY #1: COMPLEXITY, INTELLIGENCE, AND BEAUTY

"Ok Jack, as moderator I say we find a fast moving ice berg and begin our tour and discussion," I said with a sense of command.

"I see one," yelled Skeeter, "last one there's a dirty seal." They all dove into the icy blue Arctic water and one by one popped out like three torpedoes from a nuclear sub. Proving that I'm in the best shape out of the three I was the first to arrive on top of the berg skimming out of the water at a hundred miles per hour. I smashed into a piece of ice jutting out from the frozen floor just as Jack and Skeeter followed right behind careening me against the wall of ice and smashing into my bottom with Skeeter flipping up and landing on top of me with a thud.

"Skeeter get off of me. I can't breathe, you oversized sea lion," I yelled in pain. "Are you trying to cripple me? I won't be able to swim for a week!" As they all found a comfortable place to sit down on the floating tour bus, Jack suggested that I begin by laying out the format of the discussion so that we could have some "order and design" as he called it.

"Very funny, as always Jack," I replied with a smirk. "I thought it might be appropriate this year to allow Jack to begin with evidence that the universe has an end (finite) and is a beautifully designed painting created with complexity, intelligence, and beauty. It will be up to Jack to provide evidence of a finite universe, a cause, design and if possible the Designer."

"Skeeter, I want you to equally give us evidence for an unending (infinite) universe, a universe with no cause – a random fluke. If you can Skeeter, I want you to reveal the flaws of design, which would point to a macro (over a long period of time) evolution and (chance) as the creator of the universe, not a 'Designer.'

"So, how are you going to do this Jack?" asked Skeeter in the tone of a true skeptic. He then continued with a premature prediction of his opponent's defeat. "I'm going to blow your faith out of the water as fast as a sperm whale pushes air from his spout."

Jack was quick to respond. "If I were you Skeeter, I wouldn't be too quick to write off my faith just yet until you see the evidence of the masterpiece and experience the (Artist) who gives life meaning and hope. I will attempt to prove through various teleological (design) and cosmological (universe) arguments that an ordered and planned masterpiece of art, such as the universe, would logically reveal conclusive evidence for a Great Artist. I will unfold before you evidence of the Master Painter who designed the wonder and beauty of the universe. I will provide evidence of the great canvas on which He paints and the complexity of His strokes. I will show you evidence that every edge and corner of life are continuously designed to fit into each other slowly revealing its shape. I want you to observe that the pallet he uses to create color, scent, and taste are like pieces of a complex puzzle planned and cut to fit perfectly into each other. Then I will end my argument by explaining the implications this evidence would have on my faith and how God would have me live it out in my world."

ANTARCTICA: PERFECTLY DESIGNED

Jack knew he had the attention of his two friends and so he began his argument with a few local evidences of intelligent design. "I find it extremely interesting," said Jack, "how certain animals and insects along the food chain have perfectly designed features to either defend themselves or choose to be found by their prey. One example of this was discovered by a researcher by the name of Gabrielle Nevitt who noticed how certain 'birds known as "tube noses," including some albatrosses and shearwaters, use the smell of invisible gases to home in on shrimp-like krill and other food.'[320]

"Look, here comes a whole flock of shearwater birds now. Let's follow them and see if they can actually lead us to some krill," suggested Jake.

"There is also an example of "animals, mites, ticks and nematode worms (who are able to) tolerate the low temperatures in the winter by becoming frozen in ice under rocks and stone. And get this they can survive because they have antifreeze in their bodies that stop all motion and bodily functions while frozen. Then when it warms up again and the ice melts, they become active again.'[321] If this example does not convince you guys that a specific design is not in play here, you are choosing not to believe the obvious," exclaimed Jack who surprised himself with the accuracy of his quotes.

---

[320] Nature, www.pbs.org/wnet/nature/antarctica/iceboxhtml.
[321] Ibid. p.1

INSTINCT, FLUKE OR INTENSE PLANNING

The other two fell silent and Jack knew that he had to bring some examples even closer to home in order for them to understand the importance of his argument of design.

"Tell me gentlemen," asked Jack with a hint of superiority in his voice, "When you had your chicks last year and your wives left you in charge of them while they went hunting, what did you do to keep them warm and safe when the cold winds came?"

Skeeter was the first to answer and said, "Come on Jack everyone knows that we 'Penguins huddle together for warmth (and balance our) precious eggs on (our) feet to keep them from touching the ground and freezing.'[322] "It comes to us as naturally as staying under the water for 15 or 20 minutes at a time. They're not big miracles, are they?"

---

[322] Ibid.

"No Skeeter they're not big miracles," Jack replied, "however the evidence does point to some intense planning on the part of someone wouldn't you agree?

"Not necessarily," I piped up in an unexpected emotional outburst. "We instinctively learn those skills for survival by watching our elders in order to assure the continual propagation of the species. It doesn't prove someone designed us to do it, Jack."

Responding quickly Jack said, "I am not questioning the fact that all creation has some form of instinct and the ability to learn skills from our own kind, for now I just want you both to notice the complexity of planned behavior and the perfect order of what you would call "instinct." You must admit that it would be very difficult for "chance" to fluke off such precise, built in mathematical equations that fit perfectly into our universe. Take for example the gas that excretes from a krill attracting the 'Tube nose' birds to their exact location? This points to order and design Pete and if there is evidence of order and design it is logical to assume a Designer."

Jack continued on with one more example of design before he moved on to presenting evidence of a finite universe.

"One more great example of design is water" said Jack. "Water covers at least two thirds of our planet and is a very interesting compound. The amazing thing about water is that it freezes and then floats. Most other compounds do not float when they are frozen. I believe this very important element known as H2O was designed to float for many reasons. As you both know, we are floating on a sheet of Ice, which in many places protects what we depend on for food. Here in Antarctica we still have some open water, however in rivers and lakes if the ice did not float on top in the winter, everything would die. My friends Jimmy Davis and Harry L. Poe explained it this way: "As water freezes, ice forms on the surface of the river or lake. Leaving liquid water below it for marine life to exist. The surface ice insulates the water and aquatic life below. If ice were denser then liquid water, the ice would sink upon freezing and accumulate on the bottom. During the summer the ice on the bottom would not melt. Year by year, more and more ice would accumulate until all aquatic life would be eliminated." [323] "Here again," explained Jack, " we see the perfectly ordered plan of design built into essential elements of life in order to harmonize with the world around it"

"All right Jack," I admitted with an embarrassed shrug, "those are impressive arguments for design from earth, however the big question for Skeeter and I would have to be answered from space before we would be convinced everything was designed. If everything were designed then there would have to be evidence of a Designer. If He exists and He created the universe and all that is within it, there must be evidence of a beginning. This would mean that the universe is finite and proving that, will be infinitely more difficult."

END OF SAMPLE

---

[323] Davis, Jimmy H., Poe, Harry l. "Designer Universe, Intelligent Design and the Existence of God" Brodman and Holman Publishers, Nashville Tennessee, 2002, p.153

CPSIA information can be obtained
at www.ICGtesting.com
Printed in the USA
FSOW03n0943040817
37183FS